YOUR VOICE MATTERS:

STAND UP, SPEAK OUT

Susan Skog

Cliffrose Communications
Fort Collins, Colorado

Other Books by Susan Skog

Mending the Sisterhood & Ending Women's Bullying

The Give-Back Solution:
Create a Better World with Your Time, Talents & Travel

Peace in Our Lifetime:
Insights from the World's Peacemakers

Radical Acts of Love:
How Compassion is Transforming Our World

Depression:
What Your Body's Trying to Tell You

ABCs for Living

Embracing Our Essence:
Spiritual Conversations with Prominent Women

To contact Susan Skog: www.susanskog.com

Printed in the United States of America
August, 2019

Cover design by Joey Carrasco—Graphic Design

Library of Congress Control Number: 2019912554

ISBN   978-0-9758696-2-8

ACKNOWLEDGMENTS

Through its journey, many people advocated for this book, and I give you all a huge and heartfelt standing ovation. Author Laura Resau's earliest belief in this book was a perfectly timed boost. I'm also grateful to authors Karla Oceanak, Teresa Funke, Natasha Wing, and Jim Davidson for their keen empathy and support. I was so blessed to have editor Natalie Plowman; book cover/branding designer Joey Carrasco; and intern Sydney Gradisar-Jansen in my book village.

This book would not have come into being without the support of some incredible, dedicated educators and counselors, namely Webber Middle School teachers Donna Brown, Lora Bundy, Katie Sovine, and counselor April Stutter. They and the rest of their teams. Heroes all.

My love and gratitude to friends and family, here and in the Midwest, and to my husband, Jim, and son, Evan, who lovingly lit a fire in me to "do something" with my passion to help empower young people. Hugs to my sister, Joan Conrad, who proofed at the final hour. Much love to dear friends, Ted and Faustine Settle, my beloved book group, Ann, Beth, Cynthia, Gail, Lisa, Nina, and Susan, cousins Beverly Clark and Suzanne Menke, and many others, who saw the wisdom in this project and helped make it a reality with their time, talent, treasure, and "you can do this!" support. Most importantly, my deep love and thanks to the inspiring young people in this book to whom it's dedicated.

Contents

INTRODUCTION

THIS IS YOUR TIME: YOU'RE BEING ASKED TO FIND YOUR VOICE AND FIND IT QUICKLY

"There's a moment when you have to choose whether to be silent or to stand up." — Malala Yousafzai

You're living in a time when the world is listening to young, courageous voices as never before. The bold voices of Emma González, Cameron Kasky, David Hogg, Alex Wind, and other Parkland, Florida, school shooting survivors and gun control advocates.

The urgent and unforgettable voices of climate change activist Greta Thunberg, girls' education advocate Malala Yousafzai, and so many less-known, but-no-less-brave people you'll meet in this book.

All of us are living in a time when kids and young adults are standing up and speaking out to transform the world as we know it. Let them speak to you. Answer their calls, and join them. If you don't already, think of them as your tribe. Find strength in their strength. They're holding the door wide open for you to step up and find your own voice with more boldness, clarity, and power. Accept their invitation. Be the voice of your generation. And remake this world with your own passions.

Sit with and listen to all these young leaders. Soak up, as well, the "stand up, speak out" guidance in this book from some sage, contemporary leaders, like Michelle Obama, Oprah, Princes William and Harry, and others.

They and many in our generation stand with you and want to help you speak your truth.

We want to hear what you have to say. We need to hear your voice, whether you advocate for yourself or for others. So please know this:

— Your voice matters, maybe far more than you could possibly know or have ever been told.

— You have a knowing and an honesty far beyond your years that those around you, maybe even the world, needs to hear.

— One voice has power. And your voice can make all the difference in lifting yourself and the world to a better, stronger, and more connected place.

— You're living in a moment when there's way too much at stake to stay silent.

— Standing up and speaking out? Whether to help yourself or others? That is super-hero empowering. It can make you feel alive like nothing else can.

I'm so happy you somehow found this book. It's really great to meet you. I hope this book helps you far beyond my greatest dreams.

Because the truth of the matter is, you are being asked to find your voice and find it quickly. To right wrongs. Build bridges between people. Seek help. Smash hate speech. End inequality. Call out racism. Report abuse. Protect people. Bust bullying. Safeguard the planet. Change policies. Spark empathy. Spread love. Be kind. And speak truth to power.

You know this. You know this more than most. Or at least more than most are willing to admit. You're living with rising global nationalism, climate change, alarming natural disasters, naked discrimination, self-serving political leaders, heavy college debts, and, yes, tragically, the emergency of school shootings.

Closer to home, you may be dealing with bullying, family upheavals, mental illness, abuse, parents who don't accept your sexuality, school pressures, friendship stress, and more.

SOMETIMES IT FALLS UPON A GENERATION TO BE GREAT. YOU CAN BE THAT GENERATION

In the midst of all this, your mission, should you choose to accept it, is to rise up and deal with these tough realities. With your words and actions. Beloved South African leader Nelson Mandela once said, "Sometimes it falls upon a generation to be great, you can be that generation."

You can be that generation. And yeah, I know, that's a lot to expect. I wish my generation asked that much of itself, believe me. I get that a wide platform of stuff now falls on your still-widening shoulders. And you may want to shove it off. Hide. Stay silent. Be cynical. Give up.

But please don't. Because your one and powerful voice matters. I wrote this book, interviewing and gathering dozens of young voices and ideas to let you know that many of us see you and believe in you. We want to help amplify your voices and stand with you. We're here to offer what help we can so you can better tap into your courage, clarity, and power to seize this moment. You can't do it all alone, and you shouldn't be asked to.

YOU WERE BORN FOR THESE TIMES, AND WE NEED YOUR CLARITY, FIERCENESS, AND PASSION

But also know this: You. Are. Up. To. This. Mission. You were born for these times. There is no accident. Your generation possesses an extraordinary sense of fairness and social justice and heart for human rights. You don't accept dishonesty, and you often speak with integrity in a way that many adults never will. You are not afraid to be fierce when fierceness is required. No wonder you call for—often demand—change in a way that older generations don't.

"There may not be a segment of the population that expresses itself with more clarity and passion," said author Dave Eggers in an August 2, 2018, article in *The Guardian*, "Their Voices Will Be Heard: Young Writers Gather in San Francisco."

"That's why, after the mass shooting in Parkland, Florida, it was the voices of the teen survivors that ripped the sky open and commanded the world's attention," Eggers said. "Listening to Emma González's very first speech to the media, barely 24 hours after witnessing the execution of her peers, is a lesson in the power of words. She was concise, lyrical, but never willing to pull a punch. She articulated our national sorrow and fury better than anyone else. She gave us both catharsis and a mission."

Don't ever underestimate the power of your words. Marjory Stoneman Douglas's student newspaper, *The Eagle Eye*, was honored at the Pulitzer Prize ceremony this spring. The administrator of the awards, Dana Canedy, recognized the work of the students in the wake of the mass shooting at their school on February 14, 2018. "I want to break with tradition and offer my sincere admiration for an entry that did not win, but that should give us all hope for the future of journalism in this great democracy," Canedy said in a *New York Times* April 16, 2019, article, "Parkland Students Bask in Pulitzer Mention: 'They Took Us Seriously.'"

SHAKE OFF YOUR FEARS TO SHAKE THINGS UP

Canedy continued, "These budding journalists remind us of the media's unwavering commitment to bearing witness, even in the most wrenching of circumstances, in service to a nation whose very existence depends on a free and dedicated press."

Eagle Eye Co-Editor-in-Chief Hannah Kapoor spoke to your generation in an interview with MSNBC: "I would just want other students and other young people to know that their words matter, and that if you have a story it's your right to tell it. Don't let anyone else tell it for you. Because it starts now."

It starts now. Your voice matters. Do you long to rip the sky open? Rise up and demand change? Tell a harsh truth that needs to be told? Bring a labor of love into the world? Be who you are? It takes just as much courage to do that as it does to step onto a stage. I get that. However you want to stand up and speak out, use this book as lift. And exercise the power and privilege with which you were born.

And whether you're using your voice to advocate for yourself or for others on a larger platform, seek out the helpers. Lean on this book and the great people and voices in it. Let your peers, famous and not-so-famous, and some of today's most admired voices here clear a few branches on the path so you can rise up and speak out. And say what you have to say.

We all have to shake off our fears and say what we have to say. Even when it's scary and the haters or critics are at our backs.

YOU ARE NEVER TOO YOUNG TO MAKE A BIG IMPACT

Don't let anything stop you from saying what you absolutely have to say. Kick despair to the curb. Demand that things change for the better. Reach for hope. Live out loud.

For sure, these times can sometimes look like a hot, scary mess. On any given day, our inner peace can melt along with the polar ice caps. Other times, closer to home, challenges and crises, not of your own making, stare you in the face. And you have to decide how or if you can ask for what you need, maybe desperately need. No sugar coating.

Stand on the shoulders of the people you'll meet in this book. See how they found their own fierce and precious voice. And the out-the-roof satisfaction they feel from doing so.

It's time for you to feel that. To add light and goodness and shine to a world so in need of all that. Because life can be hard, right? And we often have to be the one who says what others can't bring themselves to say. Or we have to dig really deep and find the courage to speak up to protect ourselves and those we love. There's nothing tougher than regretting the things we didn't say, as some share in this book.

LET THE WORLD HEAR YOU. ONE VOICE CAN JUMP-START FAIRNESS, WAKE UP THE DECISION-MAKERS, LAUNCH CHANGE, AND BRING PEOPLE TOGETHER

Sure, some people may say you're too naive. Too unskilled. Too young. Too full of yourselves. But that's because they've maybe not heard wise voices like yours. They just don't know how to wrap their heads around young people with so much courage and truth.

Some may not have felt that same clarity in themselves. Maybe they still let their fears shut down their own voices. Without a doubt, they know your collective voices are a force with which to be reckoned. And you get stuff done.

That makes you game-changing. Unstoppable. Necessary. Powerful. Inspiring. And super influential.

Don't squander or take for granted any of that. Keep. Speaking. Cause we need more stuff done. Keep speaking, no matter your age. You'll meet kids in this book, one as young as six, who are using their voices to inspire thousands and change what needs to be changed.

The act of speaking, for yourself or others, keeps you hopeful. Helps you stay healthy. Connects you with other amazing people. Allows you to fall in love with yourself and your own true voice.

Let the world hear you. Your one voice can jump-start fairness, wake up the decision makers, launch change, and bring people together. "It only takes one voice, at the right pitch, to start an avalanche," author Dianna Hardy said.

Go out there, and spark a much-needed avalanche of love and compassion. Whatever brought you and your voice to this book, I'm so happy you're here. I see you. I applaud you. And I can't wait to hear what you have to say.

ONE TEEN'S VOICE: "As the first generation with the digital world at our fingertips, we've developed a sense of urgency in problem solving that is new to human history."

ESSAY BY COLORADO HIGH SCHOOL STUDENT SYDNEY GRADISAR-JANSEN

"I do understand how earlier generations see valid reasons for overlooking our young voices, but they are also forgetting one very important thing; my still-growing peers and I will be living on this planet for decades after our older critics have finished their lives.

"So many events are happening today that will determine the fate of humans. I worry every day about the rising temperature of our planet and every time I walk into school, I am on the lookout for anyone with a suspicious lump in their pocket because I fear it might be a gun. These are very real concerns, but we can help by advocating for these problems because future citizens of the world will have to live with the choices made by those who used their voices earlier.

"We don't want to live in the moment. We want to build a safe and lasting future. This is not to say that older adults don't have these qualities, but as the first generation with the digital world at our fingertips, we have developed a sense of urgency in problem-solving that is new to human history.

"In my opinion, this urgency is due to the fact that many of our current problems--robbing the earth of its resources for production, overlooking gun-related violence in favor of payouts, sending hateful words with the touch of a button, etc.--come from multimillion-dollar industries that took decades to build. We need to be quick to action now because we don't have decades to reverse the effects of these industries, we have only years.

"The pollution and violence of our world are speeding up by the minute, and with it, we must also hasten our response. Luckily, with the development of technology, we are able to organize petitions, protests, and boycotts in a few simple keystrokes.

"This will be the innovation that amplifies our voices like never before, of that I am sure. Aside from urgency, another trait of my peers that will prove extremely important right now is our ability to speak concisely and with candor.

"I grew up in the age of advertisements. Sitting down to watch morning cartoons meant being blasted with promotions and commercials every five minutes, and my developing brain had no way to tell which information was true and which was deceitfully tailored to make me want something that I didn't need.

"This has been present my entire life, being surrounded by screens projecting competing facts and opinions. Everything is advertised with the sole purpose of making money, so seeking out the truth is much more difficult than you might imagine.

"That is why the young people of today don't waste time or energy sugarcoating the very real problems that we face. We want to get the important information out to the public so they can educate themselves and take action.

"Some might say that this bluntness makes us rude, but we need a shock factor—a peaceful way to get the public's attention and educate it. Any kind of demonstration that includes violence will only alienate more people, so we should use nothing more than our words and numbers. We need everyone to see what is going on—the corruption, the pollution, the violence, the bullying—without any veils.

"That is the only way we have a chance of fighting it and making our planet a safer place. It's easy to say that 'the children are our future.' But what we need to do is listen to the children and the teenagers, not just leave them to deal with the choices they didn't get to make. In opening our minds and our hearts to the voices that have long been muffled, we can rise above the chaos and create a new society of peace and acceptance."

CHAPTER ONE
RISE UP AND LIVE OUT LOUD:
MEET THREE TEENS

"I want our young people to know that they matter, that they belong. So don't be afraid — you hear me, young people? Don't be afraid. Be focused. Be determined. Be hopeful. Be empowered...Lead by example with hope, never fear."
— Michelle Obama

So who's jumped on a bus or train, only to find all the seats full? You know how it goes. If you don't quickly find something to hold onto, you'll lose your balance, even fall on your butt, when the bus or train slams to a sudden or unexpected stop, or lurches and speeds up quickly. So fun. Always embarrassing.

If you're able to grab the nearest pole or strap, you can stay balanced, planted on your two feet, and get where you're going, no matter how many insane lurches. Right?

So think of your own voice like that. As life surges in an unexpected way or grinds to a sudden stop, your voice helps you reach out, steady yourself, and stay calm and upright. Using your voice helps you move forward. Confident and solid, until you reach your destination.

Here are three young people who, when their life suddenly shifted beneath their feet, chose to rise up, find firm ground, and speak.

See if you can see yourself in each of them. Imagine using your voice as they did. To stand up for what you believe, based on your own values, experiences, and life story. Imagine how it would feel if you stood in front of the world with your authentic voice and had this kind of impact. Or spoke your truth to the people who matter the most around you.

Study how each of these individuals made a choice, in the moment, whether to stay silent, or speak. Understand that any of us can still speak, even when we are afraid. "Fear" can either mean, "Forget Everything and Run," or "Face Everything and Rise," according to Zig Ziglar.

My hope is that these and other stories in this book help you stand up and rise like the sun. And keep rising.

MEET EMMA GONZÁLEZ

Seventeen-year-old Marjorie Stoneman Douglas senior Emma González did not even know how to use Twitter when her name began to explode on it. "You know that meme where it's a picture of a Grandma in front of a computer? That was me...someone DM'd me, and I was like, 'O.K, so how do I respond? Where does the keyboard go?'" — Emma González, interviewed for a March 7, 2018, *New York Times* article, "How the Parkland Students Got So Good at Social Media"3

González was trending on the social media platform after she stepped up to a microphone and spoke unforgettable truth to power at a gun control rally in Fort Lauderdale, Florida, days after a gunman killed 17 people at her school in nearby Parkland on Valentine's Day, 2018.

Before the shooting? González was the president of her school's Gay-Straight Alliance, and a tracking team leader on Project Aquila, a mission to send a school-made weather balloon into space. She has said she enjoys creative writing and astronomy.

During the shooting? She hid in the auditorium for two hours with dozens of other students until police officers let them out. No young person should have to endure that kind of terror.

Just 72 hours after the mass shooting that traumatized her high school, millions applauded when

González pulled no punches. She said what many felt, but didn't or couldn't bring themselves to say out loud.

"We certainly do not understand why it should be harder to make plans with friends on weekends than to buy an automatic or semi-automatic weapon." — Emma González

As reported on CNN on February 17, 2018, this is an excerpt from González's speech, delivered after she invoked a moment of silence:

"Every single person up here today, all these people, should be home grieving. But instead we are up here standing together because if all our government and President can do is send thoughts and prayers, then it's time for victims to be the change that we need to see. Since the time of the Founding Fathers and since they added the Second Amendment to the Constitution, our guns have developed at a rate that leaves me dizzy. The guns have changed but our laws have not.

"We certainly do not understand why it should be harder to make plans with friends on weekends than to buy an automatic or semi-automatic weapon. In Florida, to buy a gun you do not need a permit, you do not need a gun license, and once you buy it you do not need to register it. You do not need a permit to carry a concealed rifle or shotgun. You can buy as many guns as you want at one time.

"I read something very powerful to me today. It was from the point of view of a teacher. And I quote: 'When adults tell me I have the right to own a gun, all I can hear is my right to own a gun outweighs your student's right to live. All I hear is mine, mine, mine, mine.'

"Instead of worrying about our AP Gov Chapter 16 test, we have to be studying our notes to make sure that our arguments based on politics and political history are watertight. The students at this school have been having debates on guns for what feels like our entire lives. AP Gov had about three debates this year. Some discussions on the subject even occurred during the shooting while students were hiding in the closets.

"The people involved right now, those who were there, those posting, those tweeting, those doing interviews and talking to people, are being listened to for what feels like the very first time on this topic that has come up over 1,000 times in the past four years alone..."

González concluded by saying, "The people in the government who were voted into power are lying to us. And us kids seem to be the only ones who notice and our parents to call BS. Companies trying to make caricatures of the teenagers these days, saying that all we are self-involved and trend-obsessed and they hush us into submission when our message doesn't reach the ears of the nation, we are prepared to call BS.

"Politicians who sit in their gilded House and Senate seats funded by the NRA telling us nothing could have been done to prevent this, we call BS. They say tougher gun laws do not decrease gun violence. We call BS. They say a good guy with a gun stops a bad guy with a gun. We call BS.

"They say guns are just tools like knives and are as dangerous as cars. We call BS. They say no laws could have prevented the hundreds of senseless tragedies that have occurred. We call BS. That us kids don't know what we're talking about, that we're too young to understand how the government works. We call BS.

"If you agree, register to vote. Contact your local congress people. Give them a piece of your mind."

Emma González, David Hogg, Cameron Kasky, Jaclyn Corin, Alex Wind, and many other Marjory Stoneman Douglas students. We'll be reading about their bold voices for years to come.

And whether you agree with their stance on gun control or not, you can still learn volumes from them. About how they found their courage, organized, strategized, set ambitious goals, and acted for change. You can see how they gained momentum by launching the "March for Our Lives" movement and "Road to Change" tour that galvanized millions, registered thousands of young voters, and catalyzed gun-control legislation in Florida and elsewhere in the country.

According to a February 13, 2019, article in the *New York Times,* "Parkland Shooting: Where Gun Control and School Safety Stand Today," a gun control bill Florida passed "now allows law enforcement—with judicial approval—to bar a person deemed dangerous from owning guns for up to a year. Florida courts granted more than 1,000 such orders in the first nine months after the law took effect, according to Associated Press.

Eight other states have passed similar 'red flag' laws in the past year bringing the total with such laws to 14."

MEET GRETA THUNBERG

When Sweden experienced its warmest year on record with heat waves and wildfires, 15-year-old Greta Thunberg became fed up with waiting for government officials to avert a climate crisis. After researching many ways to broadcast her feelings, on August 20, 2018 this small, pigtailed child with Asperger's walked out of school to protest the fact that leaders were refusing to take any major climate-change actions. "When I told my parents about my plans they weren't very fond of it. They did not support the idea of school striking, and they said that if I were to do this I would have to do it completely by myself and with no support from them," Thunberg posted on Facebook on February 11, 2019.

When Thunberg walked out of school, no other students followed her. Undaunted, she walked over to the Swedish Parliament and sat on the cobblestoned street in front of the building with a banner emblazoned with, "Skolstrejk för Klimatet"— or "School Strike for the Climate." She passed out fliers with a long list of facts about the climate crisis and why she was striking.

Though Thunberg acted alone, against her parents' wishes, she quickly found her "tribe," beginning with a Swedish entrepreneur and business man active in the climate movement, Ingmar Rentzhog, who was among the first to arrive. "He spoke with me and took pictures that he posted on Facebook. That was the first time I had ever met or spoken with him. I had not communicated or encountered with him ever before." Greta said in her Facebook post.

"It shocks me how great a length we have to go to be heard," said 16-year-old Miranda Ashby, who'd traveled more than two hours to London with roughly 50 of her classmates. "We are protesting now because if not now, when?" — March 15, 2019 *Time Magazine*

Thunberg lit a fuse that has gone around the world and only gotten brighter. From that Friday on, weekly Climate Strikes spread across the earth. On March 15, 2019, a *Time Magazine* article, "It's Literally Our Future. Here's What Youth Climate Strikers Around the World Are Planning Next," reported on the movement in London: "Inside the U.K. Houses of Parliament, the grown-ups were at work. Outside, thousands of others — many of whom were not old enough to vote — were doing their best to make sure business was anything but usual. With their chants echoing down the streets, they were among an estimated 1.6 million students in over 120 countries who left school on March 15 in protest of adult inaction on climate change."

With famed humanitarian Jane Goodall at her side, Thunberg went on to speak at an annual event that attracts the biggest and most noteworthy leaders in the world, The World Economic Forum, in Davos, Switzerland. And at the United Nations Climate Change COP24 Conference, to leaders in the EU, at TEDX Stockholm, and many other places. Thunberg met Pope Francis in the Vatican and has addressed members of the European parliament.

"I've learned that you are never too small to make a difference." — Greta Thunberg

"I've learned that you are never too small to make a difference. And if a few children can get headlines all over the world just by not going to school, then imagine what we could all do together if we really wanted to," Thunberg said in her United Nations speech.

"Adults keep saying we owe it to the young people to give them hope. But I don't want your hope. I don't want you to be hopeful. I want you to panic. I want you to feel the fear I fear every day. And then I want you to act. I want you to act as if you were in a crisis. I want you to act as if the house is on fire. Because it is," she said in a January 25, 2019, article in *The Guardian,* "'Our House is On Fire': Greta Thunberg, 16, Urges Leaders to Act on Climate"

MEET JOHNNY HULTZAPPLE

In January, 2019, 16-year-old Johnny Hultzapple was outraged when he heard that anti-gay activist and conversion expert, Andrew Comiskey, had been hand chosen by Denver's Catholic Diocese for a highly publicized conference. Comiskey's organization aims to "heal" people it deems "sexually and relationally broken." A banner spewing Comiskey's bigotry was hung outside the Catholic event at the St. John Paul II Center for the New Evangelization. It read: "There is no such thing as a 'gay' person. That is a popular myth. Satan delights in homosexual perversion." A gay young man with a voice, Hultzapple knew what he had to do.

With the support of his "amazing" family, Hultzapple penned his first ever guest opinion, which ran on January 30, 2019 in a small Colorado newspaper, *The Colorado Times Recorder*. It read: "I AM a gay person. I AM a homosexual; and there is absolutely nothing perverted about me. In Genesis 1:26, God says, "Let us make man in our image, after our likeness." Based on Christian belief, humans are made in the likeness of God. I believe this includes STRAIGHT, GAY, LESBIAN, BISEXUAL, TRANSGENDER, or QUEER individuals. LGBTQ people are made in the image and likeness of God.

"For 11 years of my life, I attended Catholic school right down the road from the JP II center," Hultzapple continued. "In fact, I used to run around the JP II center for cross country practice. My fond memories of Catholic school are unfortunately tainted with dark and hurtful moments of bigotry–bigotry that will stay with me the rest of my life.

> **"Knowing that people cared and wanted to hear my voice—needed to hear my voice—was the biggest reward of all."**
> **— Johnny Hultzapple**

"This bigotry is often promoted in the Catholic religion, although it is not promoted by all. The ironic part of this bigotry is that Catholicism is a religion centered on love: God's love for his son, Jesus' love for his people, and the people's love for Jesus shown by loving others."

Hultzapple's guest opinion was viewed a quarter million times, and the newspaper's site crashed. He received supportive messages from people across the world on social media platforms and via emails.

"I've been printing the responses and reading them over and over again. I got messages from people at my school and other Catholic schools. Some said, 'Thank you. Way to go. I wanted to say something for a long time.'"

In an interview with me, Hultzapple said his favorite email was from a middle-aged, gay man, who went to his same elementary and middle school. "His story was similar to mine, and he said he was really thankful for me. He said I offered a 'glimmer of hope' to other gay men by being my authentic self.

"All these messages give me hope for a better and brighter future. Knowing that people cared and wanted to hear my voice—needed to hear my voice—was the biggest reward of all. It was so validating. And I will continue to fight for the love and acceptance of all people."

Later, Hultzapple was invited to speak in the Colorado Legislature to support a bill banning conversion therapy. "It was a cool experience. It felt so great and allowed me to share my voice again."

Part of his testimony: "No child should ever be subjected to the torture of being told to change that which is unchangeable. LGBTQ individuals are not able to change their orientation any more than a heterosexual person can. It is deceitful and abhorrent to suggest otherwise."

On May 31, 2019, Colorado Governor Jared Polis signed the bill into legislation, banning conversion therapy in Colorado.

NOW IT'S YOUR TURN. WHAT CALLS TO YOU? WHAT NEEDS TO BE SAID? A FEW TAKEAWAYS AND QUESTIONS TO ASK YOURSELF

How about you? Is there something right now that's calling, maybe even yelling at you to speak out, either in your own world or on a larger stage?

Emma, Greta, Johnny. Three teenagers living ordinary lives until something called like crazy, right in front of them. Asking them to decide: Stay silent or speak? Look away or jump in? Stay in the shadows or boldly step up to the microphone?

What would you have done in any of their shoes? What might be asking you to speak right now? Is there something that, even if you try to ignore it, just keeps pushing at you? What's under your skin—or right on the surface begging you to give voice to it? If you spoke your truth today, what would it sound like?

These three teenagers and others you'll meet in this book show how much an authentic, clear voice can bring sanity, hope, and shining possibility to a world that desperately needs it. They illustrate how using our voice can often be the way we stay awake, heal from, and rise above injustice, indifference, and ignorance—and even horror and grief. Our own words may be the wake-up-call that breaks an apathetic silence. Or inject love and comfort, just when it's needed.

Greta Thunberg said she was depressed about the state of the world before she began to speak out. "I felt everything was meaningless and there was no point going to school if there was no future," she said in *Time Magazine's* 2019 *Next Generation Leaders* issue.

But she channeled her sadness into action. "I promised myself I was going to do everything I could to make a difference." We can't choose what happens to us. But we can choose how we respond. We can choose to be a victim—or a voice.

> **"Whatever drives you matters. It's not too much. It's not too little... My voice and your voice carry weight. We bring our own unique magic to the world as long as we use those voices. Own that magic and sprinkle it with passion. It matters because you matter."**— **Kelly Jensen, editor of** *Here We Are: Feminism for the Real World.*

How can you take your emotions and channel them for a greater good, as Emma González, Greta Thunberg and Johnny Hultzapple did?

How can you use your feelings to get your needs met? How you feel is how you feel, and that's important. If you're sad, you're sad. Excited, excited. Anxious, anxious. You have a total right to your feelings and how you express them.

SEVEN MORE CHEERS FOR YOUR VOICE

Choose to step up. Realize you can't stay silent. Decide you have to speak. No looking back.

Use your own authentic voice. Don't try to be someone other than who you are. You are more than enough.

Forget about perfection. The only perfect thing is that you didn't shut down or go quiet.

Trust. Take a leap of faith, and trust that when you speak your truth and get your needs met, you will ignite something that needs to be sparked. Or you will set in motion a change or call to action that's long overdue.

Never underestimate your power. Never let your age hold you back. You are never, ever too young to speak up for what you know is right. When she was only six, Sophie Cruz, the daughter of undocumented Mexican immigrants in the United States, somehow knew her voice was needed. She didn't shrink because of her age.

She stepped up to a microphone at the 2017 Women's March in Washington, D.C., and said to a crowd of hundreds of thousands, "My name is Sophie Cruz. We are here together making a chain of love to protect our families. Let us fight with love, faith and courage so that our families will not be destroyed," Cruz said. "I also want to tell the children not to be afraid, because we are not alone. There are still many people that have their hearts filled with love. Let's keep together and fight for the rights. God is with us."

Cruz actually first made headlines in 2015 when she got through tight security during Pope Francis's visit to Washington, D.C. and gave him a letter asking him to protect her parents from deportation. The next day, Pope Francis spoke to a joint meeting of the United States Congress and urged greater openness for immigrants and refugees.

> **"I believe I have the right to live with my parents. I have the right to be happy. My dad works very hard in a factory galvanizing pieces of metal. All immigrants just like my dad feed this country. They deserve to live with dignity. They deserve to live with respect." — Sophie Cruz**

Try not to stay stuck in pain or anger, believing that nothing you say will matter. Don't become cynical. Cynicism isn't wisdom, but only masquerades as it, says comic and host of the *The Late Show* Stephen Colbert. This is what Colbert said in his June 3, 2006, commencement address at Knox College.

"Cynicism is self-imposed blindness, a rejection of the world because we're afraid it will hurt us or disappoint us. Cynics always say 'No.' But saying 'Yes' begins things. Saying 'Yes' is how things grow. Saying 'Yes' leads to knowledge. 'Yes' is for young people. So, for as long as you have the strength, say 'YES.'"

Say "YES." However that looks to you. Saying "Yes" is freeing, is empowering, is medicine, is expression, so it's the opposite of depression. Saying "Yes" and caring about things enough to be passionate about them can save your life. And could be a lifeline to others, too.

Say "Yes," even when you've suffered more losses or hurts than you think is fair. Loss can gut us. But don't let it stop you from saying, "Yes" to using your own life for good. Use that suffering to better relate to others and love more deeply, says Colbert, who lost his father and two older brothers in a plane crash when he was only 10.

KEEP SAYING "YES." TOO MUCH IS AT STAKE TO STAY QUIET OR ON THE SIDELINES

"It's a gift to exist, and with existence comes suffering. There's no escaping that," Colbert said in an interview in 2019 with CNN's Anderson Cooper. "What do you get from loss? You get awareness of other people's loss, which allows you to connect with that other person, which allows you to love more deeply and to understand what it's like to be a human being if it's true that all humans suffer."

So please keep saying "Yes" to what you believe in. "Somebody has to stand when other people are sitting. Somebody has to speak when other people are quiet." That's a great quote from Bryan Stevenson, a public interest lawyer, who's dedicated his life and career to helping the poor, incarcerated and condemned.

You can be that Somebody. Don't be afraid to be the first Somebody. If your Somebody stands up, it opens the door for your friends, family, and people needing you to be Somebody, too. Somebodys get so much done.

They change the world. They soar doing it. They inspire so many others, more than they can imagine. Colorado high school student Sydney Gradisar-Jansen shares how the Parkland students inspired her.

A HIGH SCHOOL STUDENT REFLECTS ON THE PARKLAND STUDENTS' IMPACT

"When I first learned about the Parkland shooting, I was in shock. I thought, 'How will our country move forward after this?'" Sydney Gradisar-Jansen said. "And then, exactly 38 days following the Parkland tragedy, I watched as 800,000 people marched in the streets of Washington D.C. to advocate for gun control. This was one of the most powerful public demonstrations I had ever seen, and I was amazed that people my age had planned such a wide-scale event.

"The massive March for Our Lives protest was organized mainly by five high school students, Jaclyn Corin, Emma González, David Hogg, Cameron Kasky, and Alex Wind. These teenagers started the #NeverAgain movement, which later planned the March for Our Lives," Gradisar-Jansen said. "They even spoke at the main march, recalling their experiences and talking about the need for change in this country.

"While the D.C. gathering was the most widely publicized, it wasn't the only rally. Over the same weekend, more than 800 satellite marches took place all around the globe in cities such as Sydney, Paris, Berlin, Rome, and London.

"About 763 of the marches were in the United States, where more than 1.4 million citizens wanted to protest the lack of regulation around guns and gun ownership.

"While the rest of these numbers are pretty incredible in their own right, I think the most powerful number that came from this event was the fact that 4,800 U.S. citizens registered to vote during the March for Our Lives demonstrations, as reported on NBC.

"One of the most common messages repeated during the marches was that the best way to make change around gun reform would be to vote for it. Along with this message, the organizers of the event set up voter registration stations with volunteers to assist so that citizens had no obstacles between them and the polls.

"As a result of this registration and voter participation, there have been many state-wide changes in legislation. The state of Florida passed the High School Public Safety Act, which raised the gun purchasing age from 18 to 21. The state of Washington passed Initiative 1639 which requires semi-automatic rifle owners to be over the age of 21, take training classes, and pass background checks.

"The state of Vermont passed several new laws which raised the purchasing age to 21 and put limits on magazine sizes. California passed a law that barred all domestic violence convicts from owning firearms. These were just a fraction of laws and legislation passed after the marches, but they are a step in the right direction toward positive change.

"Ever since the Parkland shooting, I have been amazed by these students' ability to hit the ground running and build a nationwide movement from scratch. This movement could have easily failed before it even began, but with lots of hard work, planning, and strategy, it turned out to be a historical success.

> **"As a teenager living during this time in history, I have always tried to be aware of what's going on in the world around me. Sadly, awareness won't make the world a better, safer place: action will. And these kids really did it. They made a positive impact that will affect generations to come." — Sydney Gradisar-Jansen**

"We teenagers hear the words every day: young people are the future, but I never thought much about the words until I watched the March for Our Lives. These kids really did it. They made a positive impact that will affect generations to come. By using their resources and never giving up, the Parkland survivors have become one group that young people all around the country, and even the world, can look up to and hope to follow.

"Former President Barack Obama praised the students of Parkland, Florida for 'shaking us out of our complacency,' in *Time Magazine's 100 Most Influential*

People list in 2018. 'This time, something different is happening. This time, our children are calling us to account,' Obama said. 'Seared by memories of seeing their friends murdered at a place they believed to be safe, these young leaders don't intimidate easily,' Obama added.

> **"They (Parkland students) have the power so often inherent in youth: to see the world anew; to reject the old constraints, outdated conventions, and cowardice too often dressed up as wisdom."**
> **— Barack Obama**

"'The Parkland, Fla., students don't have the kind of lobbyists or big budgets for attack ads that their opponents do. Most of them can't even vote yet,' Obama said. 'But they have the power so often inherent in youth: to see the world anew; to reject the old constraints, outdated conventions and cowardice too often dressed up as wisdom. The power to insist that America can be better.'"

CHAPTER TWO
WHEN IT'S TOO HARD TO STAY SILENT: UNPACKING YOUR ANXIETY

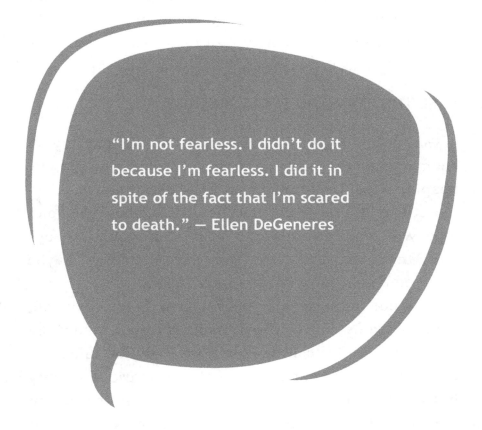

"I'm not fearless. I didn't do it because I'm fearless. I did it in spite of the fact that I'm scared to death." — Ellen DeGeneres

Let's not pretend or downplay anything. Speaking out can be the toughest thing you've ever done. Being vulnerable. Showing your emotions. Saying what others don't want to hear. Breaking the silence in the room. Being the first voice to say what everyone else is thinking. All that. All that can be super hard, crazy scary. Painful, even.

Plus, there may be few adults who can help or celebrate you. Sometimes, parents, relatives, religious leaders, educators, and others prefer you keep your head down and your voice cautious. That's what they were often told growing up: don't make waves. Go with the flow. Respect authority figures because they know best. Just do as you're told.

FEEL THE FEAR AND SPEAK ANYWAY

Out of their own shame, some adults may try to shame you. They may even try to shut you up, by heaping a blanket of judgment and hostility on you.

But trust there will always be people, young and old, who will want to—need to—hear your voice. Always trust there will be people who have empathy, maybe great empathy, for what you have to say.

Seek out those people. Ask for their help. Above all, when it's your turn to speak, make sure you take it. By doing so, you give courage to others to do the same.

So let's start to unpack some of your fear and anxiety in this chapter. Remember, as Ellen DeGeneres said in the quote at the beginning of this chapter, that fear and anxiety don't need to stand in your way from saying what you have to say.

We are more powerful than we've sometimes been told, and we can still speak powerfully, even when we're afraid. Even when it's terrifying, and we're shaking, we can keep speaking.

Tell yourself, "I can do this hard thing. I can face my fears." And then try to harness your anxiety for crazy courage, laser focus, and keep speaking. Use your never-perfect, maybe shaky voices to inspire other never-perfect, shaky voices to speak out.

Because we all have something to say. And others are depending on our flashlight of a voice to shine in the darkness, so they know just where to find us with their own flashlight voices. Love yourself enough to let your significance be seen.

"Stay afraid, but do it anyway. What's important is the action. You don't have to wait to be confident. Just do it and eventually the confidence will follow."
— Carrie Fisher

Because if you shrink, refuse to rise up big, and don't claim your power to speak, you lose a little bit of yourself each time you shut down. "Our lives begin to end the day we stay silent about things that matter," Martin Luther King, Jr. said.

And I promise you that using your voice to communicate your needs, wishes, feelings, hopes, and concerns—all that—is absolutely bedrock to claiming your life. It also gets less scary each and every time.

Learn from someone who almost let her fears stop her from speaking. When my first book gathered a groundswell of readers in the Rocky Mountain region in the mid-90s, my publisher called one day and said they were spinning my book out into a national conference series. I was going to get to speak on stage, not just in Denver, in my backyard, but also Santa Barbara, Washington, D.C., and Chicago.

I panicked and said, "Thank you very much, but I hate speaking. I hate it so much, I'd rather have a root canal every day than get up on a stage."

But fortunately, my publisher laughed and said, "Hey, we didn't know you're funny. (NO! NOT FUNNY, PANICKED, AREN'T YOU HEARING ME?!) Add that humor to your talks."

Talk about a Stand Up, Speak Out crossroads. I was forced to face my fears, and, yeah, I jumped on a stage, and then another, and another. I've now talked to hundreds of groups and gatherings, largely in Colorado, but also across the country. Met the greatest people. Had fun. Helped others. Felt the strength of my voice.

I've seen parts of the country I would have missed. Sometimes I've stumbled or missed the mark. I've had some awkward moments or events that fell short. But many times I've soared, and my message lifted people up. That's felt bone-deep satisfying in a way I still enjoy, each time I speak.

Now I'm with Maggie Kuhn who said, "Stand before the people you fear and speak your mind—even if your voice shakes."

Always remember that you can be afraid and still speak your truth at the same time. Being courageous doesn't mean fear vanishes, it means that you act in spite of that fear.

Your mouth can feel as dry as if you swallowed a bag of cotton wipes while your lips cling to your teeth like glue. Such a great look. But you can still say what only you can say. And be proud you did it.

I will always remember one triumphant eighth-grader who said, "I found out that I could speak and not throw up! I felt like I would, but I didn't!" The proud look on her face spoke volumes.

HERE'S THREE STEPS TO FACE YOUR FEAR AND SAY WHAT YOU HAVE TO SAY

From someone who was, at first, so scared to speak out she almost stayed home and missed the party:

As you practice standing up and speaking out more, figure out what helps amp your courage. Find some tools that help you find your mojo, boost your courage, and get your voice out there. Work at deep breathing. Practice storytelling and humor. Rehearse in the shower. Belt out song anthems—my favorite: *"Brave"* by Sara Bareilles. Jump up and down or dance before you speak. Use clothes/shoes as courage—who knew that gold, glittery Vans could amp one's speaking abilities? All these and more help unpack anxiety, whether you're wanting to speak your mind, one on one, or on a larger stage.

Be super, super well prepared. That helps raise your confidence, big time. And you know what has helped the most to bust my fears? Knowing that I have a message that I am uniquely meant to deliver, and if I don't speak, who will?

Realize what may be at stake if you stay silent. Sometimes your voice can help make all the difference. Try to overcome your fear to say what perhaps only you can say. Listen to Brooke Giffin's story and her message.

When Giffin started high school in Fort Collins, Colorado, she was a quiet student. According to a May 23, 2019, *Coloradoan* article by Kelly Ragan, Giffin was "a self-described 'nice' student, she didn't want to ruffle any feathers. Her sister, Max, was the advocate. Max convinced her to go vegetarian and dragged her along to animal rights demonstrations. Max was the loud, passionate voice."

The article continued, "But Max struggled with her mental health. In 2016—Giffin's sophomore year—Max, then 21, died by suicide. That's the year Giffin, now 18, found her voice. 'I feel strongly she shouldn't have had access to a gun,'" Giffin said.

Since her sister's death, "the once-quiet Giffin has led walkouts involving thousands of students, met with Colorado legislators and lobbied for bills that turned into state laws," the article continued.

"And that's only the beginning," Giffin said. "I realized staying silent makes things worse." A high school graduate, Giffin plans to study political science and hopes to run for office one day.

Study the masters. Learn from more seasoned speakers who clearly know their voices matter. I often watch TED presenters to see how people tell their story, express themselves with confidence, and share their truth to the world. Many students have told me that just watching the Parkland High School students speak out has helped them feel a lot bolder. Climate change activist Greta Thunberg said they inspired her, as well. A young woman I interviewed said Thunberg inspired her own voice, and on and on.

So read, watch, study, and try on the experiences of others your age, who stared down their fear and stood up to speak. Discover more teens like Lulabel Seitz and draft a little on their courage, knowing they, too, were scared. But rose up and spoke anyway.

MEET LULABEL SEITZ: SPEAKING TRUTH TO POWER

Overnight, high school valedictorian Lulabel Seitz of Petaluma High School in California, became one of the teenage voices fueling the #MeToo movement. During her graduation ceremony, she stepped onto the stage to deliver the commencement address in a white graduation gown with a colorful lei around her neck.

As Eli Rosenberg reported in *The Washington Post* on June 9, 2018: "Lulabel Seitz had done everything right, at least on paper. As a high school senior with a GPA over 4.0, the 17-year-old had been accepted to Stanford University, one of the most prestigious colleges on the West Coast.

"The first in her family to graduate from high school, she was named valedictorian at Petaluma High School in Northern California, an honor that was joined by an opportunity for her to give a commencement speech. But about four minutes into her speech at the school's graduation ceremony on June 2, the microphone she was speaking into was disconnected." Because Seitz faced down her fears and dared to shine a light on her allegations of being sexually assaulted.

SOMETIMES WE NEED TO HOLD UP A MIRROR TO UNCOMFORTABLE SUBJECTS

School officials had warned her not to deviate from an approved commencement speech. Seitz resisted. Four minutes into her remarks, she used her microphone to say, "The class of 2018 has demonstrated time and time again that we may be a new generation, but we are not too young to speak up, to dream and to create change.

"Which is why, even when some people on this campus, those same people..." That's when her microphone was cut. But Seitz proved, again, to be a voice, not a victim.

On YouTube, Seitz posted her version of the speech she had planned to say. That link was shared by National Public Radio on June 9, 2018 with the online headline, "High School Valedictorian's Mic Cut When She Talks About Campus Sexual Assault."

Here's part of Seitz's speech: "And even learning on a campus in which some people defend perpetrators of sexual assault and silence their victims, we didn't let that drag us down. The class of 2018 has demonstrated time and time again that we may be a new generation but we are not too young to speak up, to dream, and to create change."

In her YouTube post, Seitz wrote, "The Petaluma High School administration infringed on my freedom of speech, and prevented a whole graduating class from having their message delivered. For weeks, they have threatened me against 'speaking against them' in my speech. Sometimes we know what's right and have to do it."

Seitz said in an interview for CBS San Francisco station KPIX-TV that she was sexually assaulted by another student, and when she reported the assault to high school officials, they did not take any action.

Seitz said she originally didn't intend to bring up the alleged assault in her graduation address. But when school administrators tried to intimidate her and told her she couldn't speak about it, she knew she had to.

"They made all these rules to prevent me from speaking," Seitz told ABC News in a June 9, 2018 interview. "I decided to use the opportunity to bring it up. They told me to be quiet, told me I can't talk about it. I realized that this is a big injustice and needs to be spoken about."

As Seitz said, sometimes we know what's right and have to do it. Sometimes we need to hold up a mirror to the most uncomfortable subjects that others don't want to face to break unacceptable behaviors and toxic cycles. Silence only lets abuse continue.

So hold up the mirror and speak. When you know something is right and you have to do it? When someone tells you to be quiet? When you feel a sick feeling in your gut that others are trying to intimidate you or shout you down? When you know you have to refuse to be silenced, like Seitz? That may be exactly the moment when you should speak. Have to speak, maybe.

We are driven, hardwired, and genetically predisposed to tell our truth. As human beings, our natural instinct is to be real, honest, and authentic. Going mute to appease others or trying to swallow half-truths sucks. It doesn't feel right. It goes against our true nature. "Nothing haunts us like the things we don't say," said athlete Kevin Love, who's spoken out about his own struggle with mental illness.

Nothing eats away at us like staying silent or being a quiet bystander in the face of injustice or abuse of power.

"Every time we turn our heads the other way when we see the law flouted, when we tolerate what we know to be wrong, when we close our eyes and ears to the corrupt because we are too busy or too frightened, when we fail to speak up and speak out, we strike a blow against freedom, decency and justice," said one of my personal heroes, Robert F. Kennedy.

When you need to be, be a silence breaker. Speak and live loud, when you have to. "It's about being alive and feisty and NOT sitting down and shutting up," the singer Pink said. "Even though people would like you to."

We long to be brave. Stand in integrity. Hunger to matter. Make a difference. Crave significance. All that. The rewards of using your voice in those instances are great.

"There's something really empowering about standing up for what's right," said Susan Fowler, who has grown comfortable with her reputation as a whistle-blower. "It's a badge of honor." Fowler was the first to bring global attention to the widespread and condoned sexual harassment at Uber. She was quoted in *Time Magazine's* 2017 *Silence Breakers* issue.

"Stop holding your truth; speak your truth. Be yourself. It's the healthiest way to be."
— Tiffany Haddish

Even when your nerves want you to, don't sit down. Speak out. That's where your hero self lies.

And my hope is that, like any practice, the more you practice using your own voice, the easier and more confident you will be. I think of strengthening my voice muscles like strengthening my hiking muscles with each new mountain trail I hit in the spring, after a long, lazy winter of Netflix watching. Pushing myself to speak out, like pushing myself to reach the summit of a trail, feels much more natural with each word, each step. And the endorphin highs come with both experiences.

But first, I had to learn how to get on the other side of fear to reach that empowering place, where nothing could shrink me or keep me from saying what I have to say.

Over the years, my "stand up, speak out" muscles got stronger each time I spoke, whether in presenting to nonprofit boards, doing book talks, working with leading journalists, or stepping onto a stage to advocate for people in the developing world. Each time I shared my message, it felt more empowering.

I saw I made a difference, sometimes a substantial one. Speaking out and standing up has helped me stay strong and passionate about doing good work. It's connected me with more people doing the same, in the most honorable ways. It's flooded me with much more hope, as well, as I witness their grassroots impacts in the world.

I hope you find the same experience, over and over. Using your one powerful and authentic voice is freeing beyond measure. It's great, lasting medicine. And I trust and hope you have many adults and peers who stand with you and help you use your own voice for good. Look for them. They are there. Don't let detractors hold you back. Seek support and keep speaking.

And keep remembering that sometimes we witness or experience troubling things for a reason. Sometimes you may be the only one who sees what needs to be seen and must be said. You may spot a solution and a truth that somehow escapes people who sure seem smarter than you. In any of these instances, speak your truth. Your voice matters more than you can imagine. Let yours sing!

Here's some wonderful advice from a leading writer, teacher and TED talk leader. Clint Smith has long told his students about finding his own voice, and his TED talk about finding the courage to speak up against ignorance and injustice has been viewed about 5 million times. With his permission, it's an honor to share the transcript of that talk, *The Danger of Silence.*

THE DANGER OF SILENCE: READ CRITICALLY, WRITE CONSCIOUSLY, SPEAK CLEARLY, TELL YOUR TRUTH

By Clint Smith, Writer, Teacher, Doctoral Candidate at Harvard University, and one of *Forbes* "30 Under 30 Leaders."

"Dr. Martin Luther King, Jr., in a 1968 speech where he reflects upon the Civil Rights Movement, states, 'In the end, we will remember not the words of our enemies, but the silence of our friends.'

"As a teacher, I've internalized this message. Every day, all around us, we see the consequences of silence manifest themselves in the form of discrimination, violence, genocide and war. In the classroom, I challenge my students to explore the silences in their own lives through poetry. We work together to fill those spaces, to recognize them, to name them, to understand they don't have to be sources of shame.

"In an effort to create a culture within my classroom where students feel safe sharing the intimacies of their own silences, I have four core principles posted on the board that sits in the front of the my class, which every student signs at the beginning of the year: read critically, write consciously, speak clearly, tell your truth.

"And I find myself thinking a lot about that last point, tell your truth. And I realized that if I was going to ask my students to speak up, I was going to tell my truth and be honest with them about the times where I failed to do so.

"I will live everyday as if there were a microphone tucked under my tongue, a stage on the underside of my inhibition. Because who has to have a soapbox when all you've ever needed is your voice?"
— Clint Smith

"So I tell them about growing up, as a kid in a Catholic family in New Orleans, during Lent I was always taught that the most meaningful thing one could do was to give something up, sacrifice something you typically indulge in to prove to God you understand his sanctity. I've given up soda, McDonald's, French fries, French kisses, and everything in between. But one year, I gave up speaking. I figured the most valuable thing I could sacrifice was my own voice, but it was like I hadn't realized that I had given that up a long time ago.

"I spent so much of my life telling people the things they wanted to hear instead of the things they needed to, told myself I wasn't meant to be anyone's conscience because I still had to figure out being my own, so sometimes I just wouldn't say anything, appeasing ignorance with my silence, unaware that validation doesn't need words to endorse its existence.

DON'T LET SILENCE WRAP ITSELF AROUND YOUR INDECISION

"When Christian was beat up for being gay, I put my hands in my pocket and walked with my head down as if I didn't even notice. I couldn't use my locker for weeks because the bolt on the lock reminded me of the one I put on my lips when the homeless man on the corner looked up at me with eyes merely searching for affirmation that he was worth seeing.

"I was more concerned with touching the screen on my Apple than actually feeding him one. When the woman at the fundraising gala said, 'I'm so proud of you. It must be those poor, unintelligent kids,' I bit my lip because apparently we needed her money more than my students needed their dignity.

"We spend so much time listening to the things people are saying that we rarely pay attention to the things they don't. Silence is the residue of fear. It is feeling your flaws gut-wrench guillotine your tongue. It is the air retreating from your chest because it doesn't feel safe in your lungs. Silence is Rwandan genocide.

"Silence is Katrina. It is what you hear when you when there aren't enough body bags left. It is the sound after the noose is already tied. It is charring. It is chains.

It is privilege. It is pain. There is no time to pick your battles when your battles have already picked you.

"I will not let silence wrap itself around my indecision. I will tell Christian that he is a lion, a sanctuary of bravery and brilliance. I will ask that homeless man what his name is and how his day was, because sometimes all people want to be is human.

"I will tell that woman that my students can talk about transcendentalism like their last name was Thoreau, and just because you watched one episode of 'The Wire' doesn't mean you know anything about my kids.

"So this year, instead of giving something up, I will live everyday as if there were a microphone tucked under my tongue, a stage on the underside of my inhibition. Because who has to have a soapbox when all you've ever needed is your voice?"

CHAPTER THREE
GET CLEAR ON WHAT'S CALLING YOU:
WHAT DO YOU NEED TO SAY?

"The one thing that you have that nobody else has is you. Your voice, your mind, your story, your vision. So write and draw and build and play and dance as only you can."

— Author Neil Gaiman

So you've heard from some pretty stellar people already. Now it's your turn. If you shared what you know, speak as only you can, what would you say? What makes you so angry you have to say something? What lights you up so much you can't wait to share it? From your viewpoint, what feels smart, sane, concerning, exciting, desperately needed, or long overdue?

When it's your turn to rise up and live out loud, can you and will you be ready? Start with just the first sentence. Start anywhere.

Maybe you want to reach for a dream job, nail an audition, or go after the college of your choice. Perhaps you want to speak with more confidence at home so your family understands your world more. Or you or a friend need help or are in some trouble. Maybe you want to end a friendship or begin a relationship.

If you're a young woman, the odds are that you may want to firmly speak up and say, "I already said that!" and "Stop talking over me!" when boys or men try to pass off your ideas as theirs or interrupt you.

Maybe there's something that you can no longer tolerate. That you know is wrong and has to end.

Perhaps you see your future in front of a microphone as a change agent, helping transform the world. And can relate to this Angela Davis quote: "I am no longer accepting the things I cannot change. I am changing the things I cannot accept."

Any of these moments hinge on how you bring your voice to them. Any of these moments pivot on you standing up and advocating for what you really need. Whether that need is to improve your life or to be a ripple in the pond that connects all of us.

Here are a few young people I've talked with or read about who want to use their voice in a bolder way. All the names have been changed to protect their privacy:

- **Hannah wants to stand up to bullies in her school who tease her about her religious faith.** How can she do it in a way that won't alienate anyone?

- **Ellie knows her strengths are as a songwriter and performer and that her lyrics could help change the world for the better.** But how can she improve her writing to have the greatest impact?

- **Joey longs to be a leader, run for political office one day, and end the insane divisiveness in America.** Where does he begin? How does he inspire his peers?

- **Liv knows that a classmate is emotionally troubled, on the verge of breaking. She wants to get her school administrators to intervene and get help for her friend at school because he's on the verge of suicide.** What can she say that brings enough urgency to get her principal and others to act?

- **Josh feels vulnerable and stressed after each school shooting and somehow wants to do more.** He knows his family will support him if he gets involved in the gun control movement. They've been more concerned with each school shooting since Sandy Hook. Who can help him channel his fears in a positive, impactful way?

- **Gia wants her teachers to understand that if she doesn't turn in her homework it's not that she's a slacker, but that her home situation is in chaos.** Maybe they can't do much about her life outside of school, but it would make her feel better to speak her truth and stand up for herself. What can she say to change their opinion of her?

- **Ben really wants to finally find the courage to tell his parents that he no longer identifies as a Christian and hasn't been to church for years.** How does he say what he has to say without getting into a huge theological argument?

Hazel is crystal clear. She wants no wall blocking immigrants on our southern border. When her mother was in line to vote in 2016, Hazel leaned over and whispered: "If your generation wants to build a wall, I want you to know my generation will be strong enough to tear it down."

Sometimes, like all of us, you're finding your brave and beautiful voice because of harsh circumstances. Or because events and challenges have changed your life story. Hazel was adopted from another country. During the 2016 election she was bullied at her middle school as an adopted immigrant.

WHEN EIGHT-YEAR-OLD FLINT, MICHIGAN'S MARI COPENY FOUND HER VOICE

Mari Copeny was eight when she wrote a powerful letter to former President Obama asking for clean water for Flint, Michigan. As reported in the *LA Times* May 4, 2016, article, *"Read the Letter From 'Little Miss Flint' That Stirred Obama to Visit Flint."*

Mr. President,
Hello my name is Mari Copeny and I'm 8 years old, I live in Flint, Michigan and I'm more commonly known around town as 'Little Miss Flint.' I am one of the children that is effected by this water, and I've been doing my best to march in protest and to speak out for all the kids that live here in Flint. This Thursday I will be riding a bus to Washington, D.C. to watch the Congressional hearings of our Governor Rick Snyder. I know this is probably an odd request but I would love for a chance to meet you or your wife. My mom said chances are you will be too busy with more important things, but there is a lot of people coming on these buses and even just a meeting from you or your wife would really lift people's spirits. Thank you for all that do for our country. I look forward to being able to come to Washington and to be able to see Gov. Snyder in person and to be able to be in the city where you live."
Thank You.
Mari Copeny

Well, for anyone who says you're too young to know your truth or make a difference, look at what happened. President Obama replied to Copeny, visited Flint, and then earmarked $100 million in funding to address the city's water system.

Hoping to run for president one day and known as "Little Miss Flint," Copeny was only just beginning. She went on to create the Dear Flint Kids Project to raise money for her city and became an ambassador for the Women's March. Copeny's also spoken at the Social Good Summit and hopes to inspire other young people to use their voices and energy to make a difference, too.

She shared a few tips for any peers on fire to make a difference, as reported in a Sept. 22, 2018, *Mashable* article: "Little Miss Flint's 5 Awesome Tips for Becoming a Young Activist." I'm grateful she gave me permission to include them in this book. Something tells me we will keep hearing from Little Miss Flint in a big way.

LITTLE MISS FLINT'S FIVE AWESOME TIPS FOR BECOMING A YOUNG ACTIVIST

1) **Don't let your age hold you back. Never let any adults dull your sparkle. If they don't want to listen to you at first, keep on talking, they will eventually have to hear you out. And once they hear you out, they will see that you have a unique view of the world and that your opinion matters.**

2) Start small. Work up to big. Changing the world can start out as something small like helping fix a problem at your school or in your neighborhood. Think about what really matters the most to you and go for it. It's easy to fight for things that are close to your heart and important to you.

3) Use the power of social media for good. There are so many people out there who support the same causes that you do, and reaching out to them can help you see that you are not alone.

4) Be sure to have fun along the way. Helping others is serious and important work. Remember to take a step back every now and again to refresh, dedicating time to self-care. No matter what your cause is you still need to make time to have fun and smile. Don't take yourself too seriously all the time. Copeny says she also makes time for other activities that bring her joy, such as drawing, listening to music, playing video games, and running. And when she is working, she makes sure to enjoy herself whenever possible.

5) Never give up. It may feel like it's going to be impossible to make real change, but the hardest thing is actually just doing it.

Like Copeny, I hope you have many times in your life when you have to find the right words to channel the huge compassion in your heart for a greater good. Many of you have told me how much you love nature and animals, helping disabled students, volunteering at the homeless shelter, and supporting your family, including your grandparents.

I hope you feel your heart open, over and over in your life, with the things you love and the dreams you launch in this world.

You're coming of age at a time when big-hearted people are so needed to build new bridges of understanding, consensus, and justice—while tearing down walls, barriers, and obstacles. We need people who will throw the door wide open to more compassionate and fair practices. And fiercely stand up for others, often because others have tried to push them down.

Many in your generation will create new worlds because others have tried to force you into worlds you want no part of. Let empathy be your strength and friend.

STUDENT FINDS THE WORDS TO CREATE A LABOR OF LOVE: A SCHOOL FOR CAMBODIAN KIDS

Do you see yourself in this group? Is this your tribe? If so, to go the distance, however you're using your voice, you first have to get clear, super clear, about what it is that you really want. Here's the story of one Fort Collins, Colorado high school student who became galvanized to help kids in another country and followed her heart to make it happen.

Look at how this young woman didn't let her age stop her from making a humanitarian dream come true.

Wonder how you could do the same. Imagine what words you could choose to inspire those around you.

At this time in history, words are much more important than we give them credit for. They can inspire people to start worldwide movements, build Fortune 500 companies, and give voices to those who can't or don't know how to use their own.

When University of Colorado student Zoe Drigot was a 17-year-old Poudre High School student, she decided to help a group of kids in Cambodia. First, she had to figure out how to use her words to rally her classmates for this labor of love.

It all started when Drigot met a young student who helped her realize how many students around the world struggle to receive an adequate education. It was this small connection that sparked her dedication to breaking educational boundaries for those who struggle financially.

As part of her participation in Poudre High's International Baccalaureate program, Drigot began contacting nonprofits providing support for the education crisis. More than 260 million children and youth are out of school around the world, according to UNESCO.

Drigot decided to work with nonprofit Sustainable Schools International to help build a preschool in Phnom Penh. While this was a big step forward, more challenges were yet to come.

Drigot was told that she needed to fundraise money for the project, so she organized a Valentines' Day Sadie Hawkins Dance at her school. She knew she had to make her words meaningful to inspire her peers to attend the event. "I learned that the way I conveyed my passion for my cause moved people just as much as the logistics," Drigot said.

So she made sure that her fellow students could see her passion for her project and connection to Cambodia. Though Drigot hadn't visited Cambodia, she felt a deep bond with eastern Asia and traveled to China with her parents when she was nine, according to a 2018 SSI article. As part of that trip, she and her parents visited the orphanage in southern China where they first became a family.

"I love being able to connect to a culture. For me to really fall in love with a place, I need to feel that connection. Cambodia's just a fascinating country and now I feel completely invested, completely involved," Drigot said in the article.

As she worked to support the Cambodian school, Drigot also rallied other teens to use their voices for good, saying things like, "Love is exponentially powerful and can inspire a person to do many things." Clearly, her motivation and speaking skills paid off, because she was able to raise $2,500 to fund the preschool in Cambodia. Drigot helped provide educational support to more than 150 children.

She encountered many obstacles during her project, Drigot said. "I felt that some adults thought it was odd and not acceptable that I communicated in a respectful or professional manner because I was younger."

Drigot said she overcame these difficulties by remembering her passion for service and how this project would help others in Cambodia long after her involvement.

This story, gathered and written by Sydney Gradisar-Jansen, is a wonderful example of just how powerful words can be. How they can help one person stand up for themselves and even for others whom they have never met. It shows how you can keep your eye on your goal, even when you face obstacles or criticism.

GETTING CLEAR ON WHAT YOU HAVE TO SAY: QUESTIONS TO ASK YOURSELF

- If you could wave a magic wand, what do you believe in so much you would spread it everywhere, immediately, with a swish of your wand?
- What do you want authority figures, friends, boyfriends/girlfriends, teachers, etc. to know about you? Who are you and what is your experience?
- If you could use your True North Voice—the voice that will never steer you in the wrong direction or get you lost in the weeds—what would you have to say?
- Think about the TED talk by Clint Smith. If you lived your life as if a microphone were tucked under your chin, what would you broadcast?
- What do you stand for? Value? Hate? Love? What do you want others to know about you and what you need?
- How will you use your one, true voice for good? Do you feel compelled, even on fire, to speak out to make a difference as an activist or change agent? What solutions would you propose to end or ease school shootings, bullying, sexual violence, discrimination, the loss of species, lack of civility, or climate change? How would you propose decision makers address the

loneliness, opioid abuses, and mental health crises in the country?

- Do you want your words to inspire others to join you? What could you say that could ease someone's load, or light up a younger person or peer so much they might feel less scared and be inspired to stand up and speak out themselves?

As you get more clarity, here are five things I recommend to boost your True North Voice.

FIVE STEPS TO IMPROVING YOUR TRUE NORTH VOICE

1) First, show up for yourself. Really show up and be there for yourself. Put your phone away. Shut down all your screens. No distractions. Sit still. Get centered. Take some huge breaths and just be. See what comes up. Feel your top-of-the-world positive feelings. Listen to what feels hopeful inside you. Feel all the negative, heavy feelings sitting on your chest. Or on top of your shoulders.

Ask all your emotions, "What IS this? What are you trying to tell me?" Your True North voice is as true as your heartbeat, and it typically doesn't hide or play meek. It's often right below the surface of a crazy day, and when you slow down and tune in, it speaks. Sometimes, it whispers at first, but pretty soon, it's blurting. Calling. Maybe yelling. So slow down. Tune in. Let your voice show up. Artists, brilliant scientists, and world leaders have said that their moments of genius or "Ah ha!" often came when they got still. Einstein said,

"I think 99 times and find nothing. I stop thinking, swim in silence, and the truth comes to me."

When Marjory Stoneman Douglas High school student Cameron Kasky got quiet and sat in his bathroom in his Ghostbuster pajamas the slogan #neveragain came to him, and that hashtag launched a movement that has captivated and changed our world, reported a February 19, 2018, *New Yorker article, How the Survivors of Parkland Began the Never Again Movement.*

2) Be deeply honest with yourself. Get real about what you need and why. Maybe right now it's all a confusing jumble. Maybe so much is tugging at you, you don't know how to sort any of it out. You might be sad and angry about being bullied at school. Perhaps you long to be known and accepted for who you are—a quiet, sensitive artist.

Maybe, like climate change activist Greta Thunberg, you think adults are apathetic, insensitive, and need to wake up and do more to help the earth. What is tugging at you so much that if you don't say it you feel you will go crazy? Perhaps, you finally want to end a toxic friendship, even if that means you will be lonelier until you make healthier connections. Maybe you're on fire and inspired by a positive message or inspiration you want to share—even if your friends don't get it. Maybe it comes in the form of a song, poster, drawing, or hashtag. Many young people I've met said they feel most alive and their voice comes out when they do what they really love: their art. Try to use what feels like "home" to you to express yourself.

You may feel driven to be a voice of hope, activism, and unity, and God knows we need many more of those right now. Confidence comes when you have a deep belief that your message is needed in the world. Listen to your own voice, your own soul. If something doesn't feel right, it probably isn't. If you don't speak or say something, who will? Your unique voice is your signature, and a message that only you are perfectly positioned to deliver.

This is how Johnny Hultzapple, whose story you read about in the last chapter, listened to his voice and realized he had to speak out when his Denver Catholic Archdiocese sponsored a conversion therapy workshop: "Well, to be honest, I am super outgoing and not a quiet person, so it's always been easier for me to stand up and speak for what I want. I am the youngest brother in a family of five, I've two older brothers, so I grew up having to do so. I've never been afraid to stand out, but when it came to this, I had to speak up at a different level. I went to Catholic schools for 13 years of my life, from preschool to eighth grade.

"When I saw the Catholic Archdiocese promote this event, I was just so frustrated and angry, and I knew it wasn't enough to be only frustrated and angry. I knew I needed to put my feelings into words and do something, focus that energy, and try to make something happen by communicating what I was feeling.

"I was just so frustrated and angry, and I knew it wasn't enough to be only frustrated and angry. I knew I needed to put my feelings into words and do something, focus that energy, and try to make something happen by communicating what I was feeling."
— Johnny Hultzapple

"I sat on my computer and just typed my feelings for about 20 to 25 minutes. It all flowed so naturally. I felt this energy of what I wanted to say that had been building inside me for a long time. So it all went into this essay. Years of what had built up. Like in 7th and 8th grade, they started teaching about sexuality at the same time I was discovering that I was gay."

Hultzapple continued: "It all came together. It was a perfect storm at once when I realized how hypocritical the teachings of the Catholic Church were. It all started bubbling up inside me then.

"Like the times I questioned the Dominican nuns teaching us about this and got angry and frustrated about their response. Mostly subtle aggressions, but there were definitely times when they said outwardly judgmental and hateful things.

"Then, once I got into high school, I met more people, took queer lit and women's lit classes, and learned how to communicate in essays...So by the time the Archdiocese sponsored this event, it sparked an immediate knowing in me: I needed to stand up because what they were doing was so terrible. No one should ever sponsor that kind of event, especially a church that teaches love and acceptance.

> **"The human voice: It's the instrument we all play. It's the most powerful sound in the world, probably. It's the only one that can start a war or say 'I love you.'"**
> **— Julian Treasure**

"Was I afraid? Not really. I have such an amazing family, so I didn't have any fears or worries. I was only feeling fed up, and I knew I needed to write and send that guest opinion to the newspaper. I was more scared of the cycle continuing than of what would happen to me. At that point, I wasn't scared for myself, I was scared for all the other kids who are going through or will go through what I did. Or worse.

"And no one else was saying anything or sticking up for the LGBTQ community or saying anything. That annoyed me. If we all stand up, something can happen. I knew something needed to happen."

3) Try to get things into even more focus. As you sit with yourself, try to capture, word by word, line by line, what you need to say and to whom you want to say it. Go old-school and grab a notebook and pen and start to scribble some messages about what you have to say. Or write on your computer, if that works better for you. Don't edit yourself. Just keep throwing down some messages to get clearer. Keep scribbling whatever comes up. No judgments.

"Maybe you want to start to keep a journal or diary for your thoughts. Or paint or act in theater. Do whatever you have to do to get your feelings out so you feel rewarded, and those thoughts aren't just floating around in your mind," Hultzapple said.

And then, read out loud what you wrote. Speak it into your room. Say it with passion and conviction. Listen to yourself. How does it land on you? How does it feel? Does it sound like something you can say now outside your room?

If you're using your words to advocate for something, keep fine tuning what you write to be effective, persuasive, and authentic. Delete anything that's mean or hateful. Say what you mean in a different way. You can be meaningful without being mean. You can be passionate and powerful about what you believe without body punching anyone. Be creative.

Keep writing. Start over, if you need to. See what feels so right you have to say it. There's no time pressure. Keep listening to yourself. Aim for a natural conversational tone, not a preachy voice. Be firm and direct. No regrets. No apologies. Be fierce. Own and claim your truth.

4) Once you know what you want to say, get clear on how your words will reach your intended audience. What's the messenger for your message? In Chapter Six, we'll explore more about your strategy, plan, and tools if you're launching a cause or issues-based campaign, but here's a little about matching your message with the best messenger to reach your audience, even if it's only an audience of one.

Ask yourself, "What will work best to get my message across, knowing the audience, the timing, subject, place, etc.?" Will you write a poem, have a face-to-face conversation, start a petition, speak up at a school board meeting, create a video, or send a letter to the editor of your local newspaper? Talk with a teacher, a parent, your principal? Send an email to a journalist with an article idea about some concern? Make a sign and share its message, as Greta Thunberg did? Speak privately with an authority figure?

5) Visualize yourself as the messenger sending out your message into the world. Imagine yourself saying exactly what you want to say with total ease, strength, and rock-solid confidence. See how great that feels. Flex your fierceness, when you need to. Don't scream and yell. Never threaten or act hateful. But stand your ground and be bold and firm. Speak your truth. See people responding positively.

Imagine your hopes being realized, maybe even far beyond your imagining. Imagine all that, down to the details of you jumping up and down or hugging friends and family with relief and joy. See all that and own it.

Imagine out-the-roof happiness and satisfaction. Take it all in. Einstein said, "Imagination is everything. It is the preview of life's coming attractions." And he should know. He had quite the amazing life. Finally, look around you at people a bit older than you, who had to follow all these steps to find their own True North Voice and message.

Many young people now gain a lot of inspiration and wisdom from the young British royals. And how they found their incredibly strong and powerful voices for good. For instance, When Duchess Meghan Markle was only 11, she took on one of the largest companies in the world.

Markle saw a Procter & Gamble TV commercial for dishwashing soap, whose tagline boasted, "Women all over America are fighting greasy pots and pans." After two male classmates made a joke about how women "belong" in the kitchen, Markle said, "I remember feeling shocked and angry and also just feeling so hurt. It just wasn't right and something needed to be done," she said in a speech at the United Nations on International Women's Day in 2015.

"I don't think it is right for kids to grow up thinking that mom does everything," Markle told Nickelodeon's "Nick News" In 1993. "If you see something that you don't like or are offended by on television or any other place, write letters and send them to the right people and you can really make a difference, not just for yourself but for lots of other people."

"I remember feeling shocked and angry and also just feeling so hurt. It just wasn't right and something needed to be done." — Meghan Markle, in a speech at the United Nations on International Women's Day

Markle wrote letters to Hillary Clinton, lawyer Gloria Allred, journalist Linda Ellerbee, and Procter & Gamble, and, amazingly, the advertising tagline was changed. A month after it received Megan's letter, Procter & Gamble changed the wording of its ad campaign from "women all over America are fighting greasy pots and pans" to "people all over America ..."

Today, Markle has helped destigmatize race and class, and has given birth to the first biracial royal child born in contemporary time. She's also teamed with her husband, Prince Harry, and brother-and-sister-in-law, to shatter some of the harsh stigmas surrounding mental illness. Together, they launched initiatives, like a crisis text line, Shout, to help those struggling with mental illness. To raise awareness and empathy, revealing some of their own emotional health challenges, in the process.

Both Prince Harry and his brother, Prince William, have become heroically candid in talking about how the death of their mother, Princess Diana, impacted them. In April, 2017 Prince Harry did a podcast interview with *The Telegraph*, revealing that he sought counseling after "coming close to a breakdown" years after the death of his mother.

Prince Harry was 12 years old when Diana, Princess of Wales, was killed in a car crash. But he said it was not until his late 20s, after two years of "total chaos," that he processed the grief, he said in the interview. He realized that sticking his head in the sand, refusing to ever think about his mother wasn't helping, he said.

"Being able to talk about how you're feeling is essential to keeping emotionally and physically healthy." — Prince William in launching a new mental health campaign

"[I thought] it's only going to make you sad, it's not going to bring her back. So from an emotional side, I was like 'right, don't ever let your emotions be part of anything'. So I was a typical 20, 25, 28-year-old running around going 'life is great', or 'life is fine' and that was exactly it.

"And then [I] started to have a few conversations and actually all of a sudden, all of this grief that I have never processed started to come to the forefront and I was like, there is actually a lot of stuff here that I need to deal with."

Prince Harry sought help after his brother urged him to get some counseling.

"Being able to talk about how you're feeling is essential to keeping emotionally and physically healthy," Prince William said in launching a new mental health campaign on May 13, 2019 via a broadcast to 300 radio stations.

Prince William later talked about how the tragic loss of his mother changed him and about his own experiences with grief. In a preview for a 2019 BBC special, *A Royal Team Talk: Tackling Mental Health,* which aims to help others talk about their emotions, specifically men, Prince William said, "I think when you are bereaved at a very young age, anytime really, but particularly at a young age — I can resonate closely to that — you feel a pain like no other pain.

"And you know that in your life it's going to be very difficult to come across something that is going to be an even worse pain than that," he added.

The two royal brothers and William's wife, Kate, have created Heads Together, a charity which promotes good mental well-being. They're a fabulous example of how speaking one's truth helps others, many more than we can possibly imagine.

Is it easy to be that open and reveal your own raw feelings? In a world that still often wants to ignore mental illness or pretend it doesn't exist? No way.

As these inspiring Brits show, sometimes speaking out can be the toughest thing you've done. But it also can be amazingly liberating. It can be freeing. It can be part of your glorious journey to who you are meant to be. Do it. Take the leap. Royalty comes in many forms. Be the Queen and King of your world.

CHAPTER FOUR
CHANNEL YOUR ANGER TO WHAT YOU
LOVE

"Anger is meant to make us uncomfortable. That's how it gets us to pay attention to it—and we need to pay attention…" — Author and Therapist Andrea Brandt

If only. If only there was an app to calm anger, rage, disgust, maybe despair—or a combination of all of those emotions. One day you can feel so at peace and happy, and then the next day, you wake up in The Land of Grey. Whaaat?!

Stuff happens, your world shifts, out of nowhere, it seems, and life can get messy fast.

This chapter about anger is for anyone (and that means all of us) sometimes overwhelmed by, confused with, or afraid of anger. So much so, you may not know what to do. So you're running away, numbing down, lashing out, and hurting yourself or others.

I am not a therapist or a counselor by any stretch, and this chapter does not in any way substitute for professional help when that help is warranted. And I am a huge fan of effective counseling.

But this chapter does show you how expression can release and channel your anger so it guides your life, not controls or harms it. And how you can manage your anger, so it doesn't manage you.

The first thing to remember? Trust that your anger is meant to make you uncomfortable. There are no accidents. You are angry for a reason. Sometimes outrage is the only healthy emotion, like when the Parkland Florida students were understandably enraged—and grieving—that yet another school shooting claimed the lives of their classmates.

Anger is valuable because it gets us to pay attention to it—and we need to pay attention. We need to learn how to honor our uncomfortable, angry as hell feelings. So we move through them and then, hopefully, use that anger as positive fuel to stay awake, get clear, and do something to change what we cannot tolerate.

If you're fed up, I hear you. We all get there, at times. I get fed up many days as I read the news. Then, I try to remember to do what I know holds real power: Channel my anger for a much greater good. Follow my anger as fiercely and as powerfully as I possibly can to what I love. And then rise up and be heard.

CHANNEL YOUR ANGER AND FRUSTRATION: PROTECT AND SERVE WHAT YOU LOVE

In 2018 Black Panther star and Howard University alum Chadwick Boseman came to his alma mater to give the commencement address. He also shone a light on the graduates' love of their school and their desire to channel their own frustrations with the university to make it better for incoming students.

He acknowledged students who'd been protesting, so campus administrators would provide more housing for younger students, disarm on-campus police officers, act on sexual assault, and limit price hikes on tuition, according to a May 13, 2018, *Mashable* article, "'Black Panther' Star Chadwick Boseman Inspires Students to Challenge Discrimination."

The article said that Boseman applauded the student protestors, acknowledging their love of Howard University. "You love the university enough to struggle with it," he told the crowd. "Now you have to continue to do that ... everything that you fought for was not for yourself. It was for those who come after."

Boseman added: "The fact you have struggled with this university you've loved is a sign you can use your education to improve the world you are entering," he said.

Your generation has a lot to struggle with now, I know. My generation has a lot to struggle with "for those who come after," as Boseman said. And struggle gets exhausting. It could be easy to lose it constantly with the crazymaking, insane, and sometimes outrageous and scary stuff all around us.

I know. But don't check into the Roadhouse of Rage. Feel what you feel. And then take that frustration and anger and keep channeling it to protect and serve what you love. If you keep expressing how you feel, you can move through those feelings to the other side. To a place where you may actually be able to breathe a little hope and love into what looks cracked and broken to help make it whole again.

If you recognize and then manage your frustrations or anger appropriately, you can use it as fuel to rise up, wake others up, and be of service.

USE YOUR TALENT, SERVICE, AND KINDNESS TO RADICALLY TRANSFORM THIS MOMENT

Oprah Winfrey shared this message beautifully when she spoke to the Spring 2019 graduating class at Colorado College: "I appreciate and resonate with your class motto. The quote from Angela Davis, which says, 'You have to act as if it's possible to radically transform the world, and you have to do that all the time.' I'm here to tell you that you actually do get to transform the world every day by your actions. Small steps lead to big accomplishments..."

"So, you can pick a problem, literally any problem," Winfrey said. "The list is long. Because there's gun violence and economic inequality, and there's media bias, and the homeless need opportunity, and the addicted need treatment and the dreamers need protection. The prison system needs to be reformed. The social safety net needs saving. Misogyny needs to stop.

"And the truth is you cannot fix everything, but what you can do here and now is make a decision, because life is about decisions. And the decision is that you will use your life in service. You will be in service to life.

"And you will speak up. You will show up. You will stand up. You will sit in. You will volunteer. You will vote. You will shout out. You will help. You will lend a hand. You will offer your talent and your kindness, however you can. And you will radically transform whatever moment you're in," Winfrey concluded.

Winfrey's May 19, 2019 commencement remarks were captured in *O Magazine* and in social media everywhere.

Let's all answer her call to action. Let's show up. Stand up. Shout out. Help. Use our hearts, talents, and love to transform this world. Work to transform the moments we find ourselves in, no matter how awful and overwhelming. Try to find some blessings in the sometimes horribly painful mess. Channel our anger to what we love and keep following that emotion for a greater good.

Take a page from David Hogg's playbook. He and fellow Marjory Stoneman Douglas students and others in this book are perfect examples of teens who felt the horror and insanity around them and somehow channeled that pain into purpose.

MEET DAVID: CHANNELING ANGER INTO PURPOSE

During the massacre at his school, Hogg and others hid in a closet. That breaks my heart every time I think of it. And then Hogg started recording what he could. "The only thing I could think of was, pull out my camera and try telling others. As a student journalist, as an aspiring journalist, that's all I could think: Get other people's stories on tape. If we all die, the camera survives, and that's how we get the message out there, about how we want change to be brought about."

Hogg shared his observations in the Feb. 15, 2018, *Time Magazine* article, "A Student Started Filming

During the Florida School Shooting. He Hasn't Stopped."
As the Parkland school shooting unfolded, David Hogg
and other students hid in a closet. The shooting seemed
to go on forever and Hogg wondered if he'd make it out
alive.

The high school senior somehow had the peace of
mind in the middle of the horror to turn on his phone's
video recorder and begin speaking. "...We initially
thought the massacre was a drill. "And then we heard
more gunshots," he said somberly. "And that was when
we realized, 'this was not a drill.'"

"I DON'T WANT THIS JUST TO BE ANOTHER MASS SHOOTING"

Hogg got to his house after the shooting and was calm
enough to send his video to the *Sun Sentinel*, the
newspaper where he worked as an intern. He later biked
back three miles back to his school, shot more video,
and offered his eyewitness account to Laura Ingraham
at Fox.

At the end of the interview he asked, "Can I say one
more thing to the audience? I don't want this just to be
another mass shooting. I don't want this to be
something that people forget."

Later Hogg said, "I'm looking at the school right now.
You can see bullet holes in the windows. It's insane, and
the fact that there's more bullet holes in those windows
than bills that have been proposed and passed to save
these kids' lives is disgusting."

It was Hogg's anger—fused with his love for other kids still at risk of future shootings—that set in motion something far larger than that moment on TV.

QUESTIONS TO ASK YOURSELF: HOW CAN I USE MY ANGER TO HEAL AND HELP, NOT HARM?

Anger, properly channeled, can be one amazing and elegant force of nature. Anger, used well to stand up for good, can get things done. It helps you go from feeling paralyzed to feeling empowered. Anger, expressed for a greater good, helps you get off your bed, out the door, and moving in the world in a more energized and engaged way. So ask yourself these questions to manage your anger for a greater good.

1) What are you so angry about that you can't ignore it? As uncomfortable as it might be, what's waiting to be said, even if the words are scalding hot? It's not easy to look at our anger when we're trained to do good things that make us feel good.

"Anger doesn't feel good. It makes our hearts race and our palms sweat. It makes us feel anxious and scared. We grew up in a society driven by the 'pleasure principle'—the instinct to seek positive feelings and experiences to avoid pain. If there is a feeling we don't like, we try to get rid of it. This overwhelming urge to bury our anger—or let it erupt into intense rage—is terrible for us," says author and therapist Andrea Brandt.

But do what Brandt and so other anger experts say: Meet the anger and ask it what it wants to tell you. Try to listen to your anger, again, as if it's your friend. What does your anger call you to do or say? Use that anger, that grief, not to scald anyone, but as rocket fuel. Use your emotions to get lift and launch something better.

2) What would it look like if you followed your anger to what you love? Remember, too, that anger often bubbles up from huge sadness. Grief masquerades as anger. We're terribly sad that something has happened, and it makes us furious. "It shouldn't have to be this way!"

Listen to what comes up, and then, as hard as it can be, try to do something positive, not destructive, with all that energy. When David Hogg followed his anger to what he loved he worked to protect other young people from ever having to experience the horror he'd gone through. He also followed his anger to the feeling that he wanted his life to matter.

3) How could you overturn a damaging status quo on any issue and build change in a positive, game-changing way?

Don't just let anger sit in your path, blocking you from doing something. Pick it up, listen to it, build a strong foundation from the rocks of that rage, and then get moving. Set your heart loose in the world. Create something new that will light up the world, not throw us into deeper shadows. We need more light bearers.

When you decide to be a spark, believe me, you don't stay stuck in rage. It's just not possible. You lift off into something far greater that will serve you and your soul.

When channeled for a greater good, anger helps you advocate for others, as actor Daniel Radcliffe did. Radcliffe was bullied when he was younger, so he has used his visibility to channel his anger about bullied kids. After a shocking series of suicides by young gay teens, Radcliffe spoke out against bullying, and offered resources to teens who may be considering suicide.

CREATE SOMETHING NEW THAT WILL LIGHT UP THE WORLD, NOT THROW US INTO DEEPER SHADOWS

"Learning about the suicide deaths of Tyler Clementi, Seth Walsh, Asher Brown, Billy Lucas, and Justin Aaberg has been heartbreaking for me," Radcliffe said. "These young people were bullied and tormented," Radcliffe continued, "... [and] we have a responsibility to be better to each other, and accept each others' differences regardless of sexual orientation, gender identity, race, ability, or religion, and stand up for someone when they're bullied," Radcliffe said in an online *The List* article, "Brave Celebs Who Stood Up to Bullies."

If you're a parent or grandparent reading this, one way to help your kids channel their anger: help them engage. Take a page from Colorado State University English instructor and children's book author Todd Mitchell. When his ten-year-old daughter said, "It's not fair. Why are kids being forced to deal with all this pollution? The adults put it there. Why aren't they doing more to stop it?" Mitchell and his daughter together called Colorado Senator Cory Gardner and asked him why he supports policies that are making the climate crisis worse.

Ask questions. Use your anger for good. That's the kind of magic Harry Potter was talking about.

YA AUTHOR: SPEAKING UP CAN BREAK THE CYCLE OF SADNESS AND PAIN

Sometimes channeling our emotions for good takes immense bravery. Novelist Neesha Meminger shared her courageous story in *Break These Rules: 35 YA Authors on Speaking Up, Standing Out, and Being Yourself.* Born in a village in rural Punjab, India, in a male-dominated family, Meminger had to tune into her own knowing to break all the rules that worked to extinguish her voice. Meminger said no one encouraged her to speak her mind, question her elders, or express herself.

This is not at all unusual for girls in some countries, as you may know. But Meminger learned how to use her voice by first fully acknowledging all her emotions, even the raw and uncomfortable ones.

"Speaking up has always been about soul survival for me. When I allow untruths to guide my steps, I begin to slowly die inside. I become sad, depressed, joyless. And when this happens, I know I need to change direction somewhere in my life.

"That's when I have to go inside myself, sit quietly, and listen to the pain...Feeling the pain helps it go away. It's not easy, and it's not fun, but it's healthy. I guarantee you it gets easier the more you do it. The pain decreases in intensity and then you are bigger than it. You can manage it...But don't ignore it. Whatever you ignore keeps coming back until you face it head one. Once you move through it, instead of away from it, you become stronger, more whole—and way more powerful."

WISDOM FROM THE TOP HIGH SCHOOL SPEAKER IN COUNTRY: WHEN LIFE GETS TOO PAINFUL, REMEMBER THAT YOU ARE SOMEONE'S MIRACLE

Sometimes, things happen that are so painful we want to retreat. Hide in a zone of silence. Numb ourselves until the pain goes away, somehow. Hurt ourselves, until we feel nothing anymore. Become invisible. Turn back the clock. Fade away.

Or we can want others to hurt as much as we do, so we lash out at them. Get violent. Reject their help. Refuse to accept their love. Nathan Harmon knows all those feelings well. When he couldn't deal with his pain growing up in Indiana, he turned to drugs, alcohol, and self-harming. He became an addict and considered suicide.

After high school, Harmon was discharged from the military and racked up felonies. Some days he didn't think the pain could get worse, but it did. It really did.

Ten years ago, on July 17, 2009, Harmon crashed a vehicle while under the influence, killing the passenger, Priscilla Owens. Harmon was sentenced to 15 years in prison and was incarcerated for three years and nine months.

When he was released, Harmon vowed he would help others to make up for the loss of his high school friend, he said in our interview. "I knew I had to be a voice of hope. I knew I could empower others," Harmon said. He. Knew. His inner fire could help young people find theirs.

BEGIN BY TAKING OFF YOUR MASK SO PEOPLE CAN KNOW YOU AND YOUR STORY

He now has touched the lives of thousands of youth across the country. Harmon brings a message of hope, empowerment and out-the-roof positivity as the most sought-after, high school speaker across the country with his Your Life Speaks programs.

After spending a morning or afternoon with Harmon's message and energy, teens say they feel lit up with new purpose, fire, and passion. And they say they want to stay alive and make their lives count. How does Harmon make this happen? What does this mean for you as you read this book?

One idea Harmon wants you to consider: Take off your mask. Consider being more vulnerable. Know, really know that you're not alone, and anything you're experiencing is similar to what your peers are experiencing, he said.

"Realize that everyone is beautifully broken in some way, and being vulnerable enough to ask for help is a sign of strength. Take off your mask and use your voice—even if you're screaming—to tell your story, to talk, to communicate, to ask for help so you know you're not alone. Young people think, 'I'm the only one like this.'

REALIZE THAT EVERYONE IS BEAUTIFULLY BROKEN IN SOME WAY, AND BEING VULNERABLE ENOUGH TO ASK FOR HELP IS A SIGN OF STRENGTH

"They think they are all alone in their social and emotional struggles. They feel they are the only one self-harming, or the only one struggling and feeling awkward, ugly, fat or suicidal. They feel they are the only one driven by fear, and that if they talk about their struggles, others will look at them as different or weird.

"But I help them see that 90 percent of their friends are all struggling with the same damn problem.

"Yeah, on social media, everyone looks successful. Everyone looks as if they have a huge fan base. I help kids see that everyone is struggling and beautifully broken in some way, and if they fight their depression and anxiety and refuse to let emotions run and control their life, they win."

If you are reading all this and still wanting to stay silent? Here's a final message from Harmon: "Remember and realize that you are someone's miracle.

What you are struggling with, someone else around you is struggling with right now. And the more you can share and tell your personal story, the more they will realize they are not alone.

"The more you overcome these challenging times with your inner adversity, the more you can show, 'I made it out of the fire.' And your story will be someone's miracle and help them get out of the fire."

And as you tap into your inner strength even more, help others find theirs, Harmon said. Be a spark to help them find their own. Begin by doing kind things for others. Help them know they matter.

When you yourself begin to give away those random acts of kindness and go out of your way to encourage others and give away your love, you will feel better. You will feel your own value. You will feel your absolute purpose. You will feel more empowered, knowing you made the day better for someone else, Harmon said.

"Students tell me, 'I looked in the mirror. I knew then I had a purpose.' I know life can be tough. But when you know your life matters to others, you can walk out of school and begin to tackle whatever life throws at you."

Harmon spoke to more than 240 schools in the United States in 2019. He believes that every student he speaks to is "just one moment away from their life being radically changed for the better. When I talk with students and let them know that they matter and have worth, there is nothing more rewarding than seeing the fire in their eyes ignite," he said.

"I've gotten about 500 to 600 emails in the last four years from students who were self-harming and/or considering suicide who say, 'I want to live now.'"

CHAPTER FIVE
IN CASE YOU FORGET:
ONE VOICE REALLY DOES MATTER

"This is the moment when we either turn up the light within ourselves or move further into the darkness. Stop giving energy, time, and power to negativity. Counteract it with goodness. Notice where there is need, then do whatever you can to help..." -- Oprah Winfrey

When you're using your voice for good and setbacks happen or you get tired and discouraged, it's super easy to give up. Get fed up. Cynical. Cave. Convince yourselves that your one voice doesn't count, anyway.

Who are we to believe we're actually strong or powerful enough to make a difference? Well, actually, you have EVERY reason to believe that one person matters. It may be the only thing that matters, sometimes. We have countless, incredible examples throughout history of how one person—just one—set something new in motion.

Remember this. And use this chapter to pump yourself up a bit. It's not easy to be the one who stands up and speaks out. It can take tremendous inner fire and outer courage. So hug yourself. Ask others for hugs.

> **"It takes only one candle to light a whole room of darkness. People think, 'Oh, I have no power to change the world.' But we are the world, through our families, our work, our communities. And how you treat every person in your world has an impact on the macrocosm. Don't underestimate your power. Hate is potent, but so is kindness. And goodness, and grace. Use yours generously."**
> **— Oprah Winfrey**

Give yourself a standing ovation. Really, stomp your feel and clap your hands like you're a crowd of a million. Feel the love and hear the cheers from others. Go wild with knowing how powerful you are. Feel that groundswell. Love yourself for being so incredibly brave.

And then keep reminding yourself that change always happens with one person. One person is powerful beyond measure because if you stand up and speak out, you open the door wide for others to do the same.

It takes the first hand on the door knob, though, to fling the door open—maybe lean into and shove it open, hard. Be that hand. Be that voice. Then, others will follow. Sometimes you won't believe how many will follow.

SPEAK FOR THOSE WHO DON'T HAVE A VOICE. IF YOU HAVE SOMETHING TO SAY, SAY IT

Look at all the people you have met so far in this book. One by one by one. They changed a piece of the world, maybe a lot of it, when they spoke their truth.

And if people say you're too young to matter, well, think of Malala Yousafzai. She started speaking out about the need for girls to be educated in Pakistan when she was only 11, and is now known for just her first name all across the world. She gives great voice to many still-voiceless girls in regions where girls are prevented from getting an education.

"I speak not for myself but for those without voice... those who have fought for their rights...their right to live in peace, their right to be treated with dignity, their right to equality of opportunity, their right to be educated," Malala said. With that one quote, her voice circled the world.

If someone says you're too naive, remember Greta Thunberg, the 16-year-old climate change activist. There's nothing naive about her results. She inspired students everywhere to march in climate strikes. She inspired the governments in the United Kingdom and Ireland to declare a climate emergency.

Around the same time, a UK parliamentary committee also recommended that the country adopt a target of net-zero emissions by 2050, which would give the UK the most aggressive climate target in the world. In Germany, Chancellor Angela Merkel cited the school strikes as one of her reasons for backing a European Union-wide target of reaching net-zero greenhouse gas emissions by 2050.

No one can dispute that Thunberg is a planetary force.

Keep reminding yourself that one leads to many, sometimes a flood of many. And again, don't shut down if people say serious issues should be left to adults. Too many adults now are too afraid to speak out about anything. Unfortunately, that's the reality in some of the world.

Too many adults will not have the honesty and bravery of people in your generation, like Parkland student and March for our Lives Co-Founder Cameron Kasky, who recently tweeted: "How DARE you tell me I'm 'too young' to talk about sensible gun reform when you haven't been in a SINGLE production of Little Shop of Horrors."

Some adults will mock your courage because they're too afraid themselves to challenge the status quo. They are terrified to speak out with power and authority. Many learned this behavior decades ago. They were conditioned to believe they would be punished if they spoke out boldly and bravely. Or they've grown apathetic, tired. So even when something intolerable or horrifying happens, they stay silent. Don't learn this behavior. Don't model the silence. If you have something to say, be sure you say it.

TEENAGE ENVIRONMENTAL LEADER GIVES THE YOUNGEST GENERATION A VOICE: "THE POWER COMES FROM US"

Learn from role models like teenager environmental activist Xiuhtezcatl Martinez, who was also told that his opinion didn't matter over the years. Author of *We Rise* and leader of the Earth Guardians movement, Martinez didn't listen to anyone who thought he was too young, just one voice, and not worthy of speaking truth to power.

He refused to accept the idea that young people couldn't be part of the climate change conversation. So Martinez made it happen—beginning at the age of six when he began speaking around the world. Now 18, he has addressed the United Nations five times and is one of the 21 kids suing the federal government over climate inaction, according to an online *Grist* article, "Xiuhtezcatl Martinez Gives the Youngest Generation a Voice."

Martinez, who is half-Aztec and lives in Colorado, has been part of a group of teenagers who sued the federal government over climate inaction. He's organized protests and tree plantings and rallied youth to participate in the 2014 Climate March in New York City and the Native Nations Rise March on Washington.

This generation has to take action fast, Martinez said. "We're not just the future," he says. "We're also here right now."

"The power to make a difference does not come from political leaders or presidents or Congress. The power comes from us—the people. And our generation is rising to protect the earth and create the world we deserve to inherit." — Xiuhtezcatl Martinez

One of his main messages? Don't keep looking around for "the leaders." They may not exist. "We are the leaders. The people are the leaders," Martinez said.

He has also said, "The power to make a difference does not come from political leaders or presidents or congress. The power comes from us—the people. And our generation is rising to protect the earth and create the world we deserve to inherit."

In his first talk to the United Nations, he proved that. "I stand before you representing my entire generation," he said. "Youth are standing up all over the planet to find solutions. We are flooding the streets and now flooding the courts. We need you to take action. We are all indigenous to this earth."

He continued, "What's at stake right now is the existence of my generation. In the last 20 years of negotiations, almost no agreements have been made on a bonding climate recovery plan."

Where does Martinez' passion come from? He focuses well on what he loves, his "beautiful, magical connection to the world around me. I looked at the mountains and the rivers and forests of Colorado and I saw that as my home. I belong to them more than they belong to me, which meant understanding that I had to protect them at any cost. That's where the activism came in.

"We're tearing our world apart, destroying those things that make our world sacred. That thrust me into action. That passion told me there was nothing else that I could do but take action," Martinez said in a July 13, 2015 interview with *Rolling Stone,* "Meet the Teenage Indigenous Hip-Hop Artist Taking on Climate Change."

YOU HAVE A RIGHT TO YOUR VOICE AND STORY: WISDOM FROM A YOUNG WRITER AND AUTHOR

As you work at trusting even more the power of your own voice, here's a great essay by Marisa Donnelly. Let it remind you of your right and your power, as one person, to speak. This piece originally appeared in *Thought Catalog* in October, 2017. Donnelly is a writer, editor, writing coach, and founder of Be A Light LLC:

"You have a right. To this life. To your skin. To your body, your hopes, your dreams.

"You have a right. To believe. To stand. To sit. To chase. To embody the very values you believe in.

"You have a right. To tell your story. To be heard. To be bold and fearless and unafraid.

"You have a right. To be respected and loved and encouraged. To be noticed and empowered and strengthened by the people around you, every step you take.

"Dear woman, dear man—this life is too short to forever hold yourself back, worried about what he or she will say. You cannot always be so cautious, so conscious of the way your thoughts may shape the perspectives around you. Forget the rest of the world for once.

"Stop holding yourself back to let others say what they need. Sometimes what you long to speak is important. You are not meant to always quiet the power coming from your mouth.

"No, don't let your voice restrict the words around you. There's a fine line between speaking and shouting, between letting your voice rise and drowning out anyone who dares to open their mouths. You don't have to stand here and scream. You don't have to kick and push and be a big mess to be noticed. You don't have to change parts of yourself to attract attention.

"You just have to know that your voice is important and worthy of being listened to. And people are listening."

Always remember: If you speak out, you may just help others muscle past their anxieties or fears and go to a higher place. And grab onto hope.

"Struggling souls catch light from other souls who are fully lit and willing to show it. If you would help to calm the tumult, this is one of the strongest things you can do," says author Clarissa Pinkola Estes.

HOW A YOUNG AUTHOR BRILLIANTLY USED HER OWN VOICE TO SILENCE BIGOTRY IN A NYC SUBWAY CAR

And don't forget to use the creativity your generation is known for as you express yourself. I love how author, educator and writer Onnesha Roychoudhuri used her voice in a playful song to drown out hate on a NYC subway. The author of *Marginalized Majority: Claiming Our Power in a Post-Truth America,* Roychoudhuri is Indian-American. She is used to people asking her "What are you?" she wrote. With humor she says, "I'm human by way of California, Connecticut, then North Carolina."

But one day on the train, Roychoudhuri felt she had to do more when bigotry rose up right in front of her. Look at what she did. Sometimes it takes a little imagination to take back the room--or subway car. With her permission, I share this excerpt from Roychoudhuri's 2018 book.

"It was my uncle Bill who I was thinking of when, one day recently in Brooklyn, a man boarded my subway train and let loose an impassioned and bigoted tirade. My fellow New Yorkers did their job of ignoring him admirably, but he didn't keep up his end of the bargain, which was to move on after a few steps and pester the next car down.

"I told him that if he wouldn't stop talking, I would start singing so I no longer have to hear him." — Onnesha Roychoudhuri

"After fifteen minutes straight of his proselytizing, some passengers told him to shut up. He wouldn't. Some tried reasoning with him. But here's the thing about narcissistic ideologues: they don't respond to logic, or dissuasion in the name of facts or reason. We could fact-check him all day and night, but he wasn't playing by the rules of the game.

"In that moment, I wrestled with a familiar feeling of resignation and powerlessness. I closed my eyes in the stuffy train and thought to myself: *It'll be over soon.* But I was tired of allowing the loudest and most bombastic among us to take control by default.

"I decided that if the man would not shut up, the only way to improve the situation would be to make it so we no longer had to listen to him. I told him that if he wouldn't stop talking, I would start singing so I no longer have to hear him.

"He kept talking. So I sang.

EVEN IF SHAKY AND A LITTLE OFF-KEY, FIND YOUR VOICE TO RECLAIM THE WORLD YOU WANT

"The first round of *'Row, Row, Row Your Boat'* was shaky and a little off-key. It was all I could muster. But a few people joined in the next round, and by the third, everyone on the train was singing robustly—including a couple of kids in strollers who clapped their hands in glee.

"The proselytizer tried to get loud, we got louder. Suddenly, we were no longer the audience for a hateful man. He got off at the next stop, yet we kept singing for a few more rounds, smiling at each other and enjoying the simple joy of the reality and world we'd reclaimed."

That is such a joyful, brilliant story. Sometimes the greatest thing you can do for yourself and the people around you is to believe in yourself, without question. Believe in your voice. Believe in others joining in. Believe in the beauty of this world, though it may be buried at times.

Marisa Donnelly's inspiration, once again: "You must speak up. When you feel your heart calling you to. When the world is crashing in. When you, or someone you see, is being burdened unfairly. When there is simply nothing else to do than to let the words flow from your lips.

"Speak and be noticed.

"Speak and be heard.

"You do not have to step on anyone's toes to share your perspective. You do not have to dim another's light to let yours shine boldly. You do not have to put on a mask, a façade, just to push forward, to prove your strength.

"You are strong in your simple existence. In your laughter. In your smile. You are strong in the way you carry yourself, in the way you step, in the way you continue, day after day.

"You don't always have to be loud to be heard.

"But you shouldn't be silent.

"Speak up. Speak with confidence. Speak for what you believe.

"Do not silence your voice so the world can be heard; you are a part of this world. Speak up."

Sometimes it's up to us alone to try to claim the world we deserve. And live as authentically as we are meant to. I hope this book makes that far easier and far less lonely. I hope it helps to read the stories of others who also had to claim the life they deserve.

"Gay High School Quarterback Finds New Passion at Michigan State as Sports Broadcaster, Referee" said a June 4, 2019, headline on the website, *OutSports*. In the article, Eric Bach's powerfully described his struggle with sharing his secret of being gay as a high school football and basketball player.

Bach was around football growing up in Coldwater, Michigan since he was in diapers. He was the starting quarterback of his high school football team and the starting catcher of his baseball team.

SOMETIMES YOUR VOICE IS THE KEY THAT UNLOCKS YOUR AUTHENTIC LIFE

But friends and teammates wondered why Bach didn't date girls. He felt that people around him didn't know him completely. His anxiety and loneliness mounted. "It's amazing how the human body can be so affected by typing, speaking or even thinking about certain words,' Bach said. "You can have butterflies, instantly start sweating, and be short of breath just thinking about telling someone two words. For me, those two words have always been 'I'm gay.'"

On top of that, Bach had to put up with ugly slurs, like "faggot," at practice or in the locker room. "I knew that the slurs were not directed at me, but I could not help the anxiety that came every time I heard someone use one of those words. I was convinced that if someone found out my secret, my life would be ruined."

Eventually, Bach came out to his family and some trusted friends, and experienced "one of the most liberating and strengthening feelings. For my own sanity, I wish I would have come out sooner," he said.

Coming out was one of the best decisions of his life, he said. "Athlete. Broadcaster. Referee. Whatever path I end up following, I hope the world I live in is a world where the label of 'gay man' does not disqualify me from doing anything I want to do in this sports life. (There are very few openly gay broadcasters in the sports world today.)

"I'm proud of the person I've become and the life that I lead and my hope is to inspire others to chase their dreams while being true to themselves. For the first time in my life, I know I am," Bach said.

Bach, 20, will graduate from Michigan State University in 2021. He studies journalism with a minor in sports journalism. He works for the Big Ten Network Student U and is one of the MSU student coordinators for intramural referees.

CHAPTER SIX
YOU CAN DO IT! LAUNCH YOUR
CAUSE:
CREATE AN INTENTION AND
LONG-TERM STRATEGY

"A burning purpose attracts others who are drawn along with it and help fulfill it."

— Margaret Bourke White

This chapter is a step-by-step roadmap for those who want to use their voice to advocate for a cause or issue on a larger scale with some organization and strategic planning. I know! Woo hoo! The super fun part of the book for which you've been waiting. I get it. I can see the eye rolls and hear the long yawns. It's a lot more exciting just to get out there and DO something.

But keep in mind. "You don't change the world with the ideas in your mind, but with the conviction in your heart," Bryan Stevenson said. And you can't spark change with either your mind or heart unless you've got a rock-solid strategy and some concrete planning.

I know if you're reading this chapter you are likely anxious to speak out, act, and shine a light on your issue. But if you want to move the needle on your cause, you have to carve out time and energy so you can be smart, organized, and go the distance. And truly move that needle—not get stuck in the status quo. Or sputter out before your fire has even been lit.

"Admittedly, this pre-planning stuff is not the most fun, and being strategic can be hard when you are Just. So. Mad," KaeLyn Rich said in her book, *Girls Resist: A Guide to Activism, Leadership, and Starting a Revolution.*

But when people are fed up, one of the first things they often do is protest before picking a long-term strategy, she added. "And that's not always a bad thing, especially when protests rise up in immediate and direct response to something egregious. Throughout history, protests that grew organically from the anger of the people being marginalized have helped spark national dialogues and long-term change movements."

But without a long-term strategy, protests can end up just being one-off events. "It'll feel good for riling up your activist spirit, but it might not change anything," Rich said.

Strategies, planning, and goals help you stay super strong, run the long race, get across the finish line, create change, and yes, work in a more professional and practical manner.

They also help you measure and capture your results and successes. Even the Parkland activists were advised on the mighty wisdom of planning by Oprah Winfrey. "You can't just go out there and march," Winfrey told the students, "There has to be a very clear intention behind what you're doing and why you're doing it."

She also pointed out that by the time Rosa Parks sat down on the bus and refused to give up her seat to a white passenger in 1955, she and others had been planning the arc of their work for a long time.

So here are 10 steps to help you go the distance in advocating for the issues about which you care. They can also help you be an inspiring change agent offering much-needed solutions—not just a critic on the sidelines.

TEN STEPS TO HELP YOU ORGANIZE YOUR CAUSE CAMPAIGNS

— **Get clear on your vision. What words / messages will call people up and inspire them?** How will they be conveyed? With videos, images, calls to actions, posters, and other tools to reach your target audience, decision makers, the media, and others? Get clear on what you want to say and create key talking points to help you stay on message.

Remember to speak with heart. Share how you feel about your topic and weave in examples or stories from your own life that explain why this issue is so meaningful to you.

When I was advocating for girls to stay in school in the developing world, not get trapped in early marriages, or drop out of school to fetch water all day long, one of my calls to action that struck a chord around the world: "Girls Should Carry Books Not Water." For inspiration, research how others have expressed themselves to advance a cause.

— **Keep rewriting until you love what you read. Be bold, passionate, authentic.** And don't forget to add a little humor or lightness, if needed. Your goal is for your message to create some buzz and be passed on, person to person. Actor and activist Matt Damon has used humor to advocate for safe water and toilets for those around the world. Unsafe water kills millions each year. Billions have no access to safe toilets.

But many tune out if the message gets too serious, right? So Hollywood star Damon smiled and put a toilet seat around his neck World Toilet Day 2014 to call attention to the fact that 1 in 3 around the world have no proper bathroom to use. More tuned into his message because he added a little levity.

Another example? The Westboro Baptist Church shows inconceivable hatred to gay people with protest signs like, "God Hates Fags," so demonstrators have sometimes brought the humor in their own signs to defuse the tensions, and shine a light on how truly misguided homophobia really is. Counter demonstrators have sometimes held signs like, "God Hates Signs" and "God Hates Figs," according to an online Care2.com article, "Protests That Use Humor to Make a Point."

— Team Up. Identify your tribe: Choose your team members and get clear on their roles and strengths. Who's able and willing to stand with you? Once your message is clear, figure out who will align with your cause and go into the trenches with you. Who will serve as organizers, speakers, fundraisers, publicists, food run people, database and accounting foot soldiers, family, friends, logistical support, etc.?

Who can work shoulder-to-shoulder with you over time? Secure your event venues? Edit and proofread your social media posts? Offer moral support and humor when things get harder or help you celebrate some wins?

As wonkish as it may sound, make a transparent, shared plan with clearly spelled-out roles, steps, and a calendar of commitments and deadlines, so everyone can be on the same page. And work as a fired-up, high-energy, unstoppable team with a shared mission and free of arguments, drama, or confusion. Be powerful. Be smart. Go!

— Define what success looks like to you. What specific actions do you want others to take and what results do you hope to see?

It's way easy to be a critic. It's much harder to advocate for and present real solutions. Be someone who offers change through solutions. Set big intentions. Dream big. Someone has to, right?

Imagine others running with and implementing your solutions beyond your wildest dreams. Set a clear and inspiring vision of what you want to accomplish. Let your team all feel part of something exciting—that's one great and wonderful feeling.

For instance, by the time the March for our Lives occurred, the Marjory Stoneman Douglas students already had three primary demands: Pass a law to ban the assault weapons; Stop the sale of high-capacity magazines; Implement laws that require background checks on all gun purchases, including online and at gun shows.

They also set an ambitious goal to boost youth voter turnout. Because they were organized, focused, and enlisted a lot of support, the Parkland students were also clear that they intended to spark a movement.

The students organized rallies, town halls, and voter registration drives, often in places affected by gun violence. Other stops focused in on areas of the country with particularly strong NRA support, which activists say gives them the opportunity to have a productive dialogue ahead of the elections.

The Summer of 2018 tour, Road to Change, made more than 50 stops in over 20 states. I will never forget the electrifying energy and massive turnout at the Denver gathering. A group of Road to Change leaders also organized a separate tour specifically for Florida, where they have visited all 27 congressional districts.

— Spell out strategies and steps you will use to communicate your vision and reach for your goals.

Play to your strengths here, and lean into the skills and talents you and your team already have. By no means do you have to have a platform as wide ranging as the Parkland students did. But you do want to get clear on what steps you can do comfortably and well with your collective time, talent, and resources.

Will you speak at a large meeting? Write an essay for the local paper? Use photos and captions on Instagram to inspire action? Go door-to-door with a petition or meet with political leaders? Create an unforgettable video with a call to action? Seek press coverage? Meet with politicians for a one-on-one conversation over lunch? Launch an exciting social media campaign that ignites cheers across the world? Perform a song and pop it up on YouTube? All or a little of this?

In 2017, the *New York Times'* Editorial Board called on the Trump administration to preserve Deferred Action for Childhood Arrivals, a program that temporarily shields some young immigrants from deportation and allows them to work legally. The paper featured stories from young immigrants who were spared from deportation and permitted to work during the Obama administration.

Carlos Adolfo Gonzalez, an advocate for immigrant rights and education equity, used that opportunity to communicate his vision, dreams—and fears of deportation—in a guest essay. Study how he used his words in this piece to reach readers all over the world.

"I am 25 years old, have two master's degrees, and an inconsolable desire to contribute to the country that has given me so much. Yet, I feel fear creeping back into my life. These next couple of years will be pivotal for me. I will not return to the shadows." — Carlos Adolfo Gonzalez

"Fear enshrouded most of my life since my mother brought me from the Dominican Republic to Pennsylvania for schooling at the age of eleven. Fearing that my family's sacrifices would be in vain, I treated every test and writing assignment like my life depended on it.

"Despite excelling academically, I graduated high school uncertain of where I would be able to continue my education. For years I struggled to afford tuition at my local community college. Finally, Amherst College embraced me. On campus, I felt safe. Still, every night I closed my eyes fearing that my education would one day be rendered useless.

"The summer President Obama announced DACA I was completing a community organizing internship in Chicago. For the first time in my life, I finally felt free to pursue my dreams and use my intellect without fear.

"After graduating college summa cum laude, I helped mobilize unlikely voters in Chicago. I then collaborated on federal legislation to increase access to English language courses as a congressional fellow in the U.S. House of Representatives.

"After that, I returned to Pennsylvania to assist refugees become economically self-sufficient and advocated for the state DREAM Act. I have also continued my education at elite institutions around the globe as a Gates Cambridge Scholar in the United Kingdom and a Schwarzman Scholar in China.

"Now, President-elect Trump has vowed to rescind President Obama's executive orders on immigration. I am 25 years old, have two master's degrees, and an inconsolable desire to contribute to the country that has given me so much. Yet, I feel fear creeping back into my life.

"These next couple of years will be pivotal for me. I will not return to the shadows.

"Those who encourage me to seek refuge in another country fail to see that my desire to stay in the United States is no longer motivated by economic opportunities. The United States is my home. It is where I feel the most comfortable.

"I want to appeal for help to Americans on the fence concerning this issue. Americans who recognize the positive impact DACA has had on the lives of people like me and on the communities in which we exist. Those who are angered by the thought that American stories of people like me could end prematurely, but who have not lifted a finger to protect us, I implore you to join our struggle!"

— Identify your partners. How can you gather strength, numbers, and momentum for your cause with kindred people and groups?

Who can help you get a groundswell of supporters? Who can you rely on to take your cause to a higher level? Who are the people who may be drawn to your message, goals, and cause? Who can help you get lift and impact? Identify your donors and your influencers.

Research and enlist youth groups, businesses, service clubs, politicians, churches, civic organizations, schools, campuses, fraternities and sororities, influential, high-profile people, newspaper advisory boards, and your neighbors. How can you gather strength, numbers, and momentum for your cause with kindred people and groups? Who can help you grow your community and base?

Who can you rely on to help you be a change agent— right where you are, maybe right in your school? Are there already people drawn to your message, goals, and cause with whom you can align?

16-YEAR-OLD ENLISTS UNICEF TO HELP HER LAUNCH AN ANTI-BULLYING PROGRAM IN HER SCHOOL

Sixteen-year Snezana Dzogovic wanted to be a change agent in her own school in Kosovo and end bullying. With permission, I share this story by of how she partnered with the global organization, UNICEF, to make that happen. It shows how you can partner with a global movement to make change, right where you live each day. Dream big. Look for the helpers.

This article, "Peer Mediators in Kosovo (SCR 1244) Help Keep School Safe for Everyone," was written and shared by Chulho Hyun Regional Chief of Communication for UNICEF's Regional Office for Europe and Central Asia.

Sixteen-year-old Dzogovic vividly remembers when her classmates started to bully her. She was in sixth grade at her school in Mitrovica, northern Kosovo.

> **"I went 'into' myself and did not talk to anyone about it. I started avoiding school. My grades fell because I did not go to school. I could not study at home."**
> **— Snezana Dzogovic**

Dzogovic said the bullying started when she began listening to rock music and dressing differently than the other girls. She liked bands like Nirvana and Guns n' Roses and she cut her hair short.

Verbal and physical abuse followed. Her classmates would damage her belongings when she wasn't looking. One day Dzogovic came home with her backpack and books ripped and her mother asked her what had happened.

"When I started to talk, my mother felt shocked and embarrassed that I had not shared it before. My mother went to school and spoke to the class teacher, but she (the teacher) avoided resolving the issue," Dzogovic said.

VIOLENCE: AN EVERYDAY REALITY FOR MILLIONS

According to a new report released by UNICEF in 2018, *Violence in Schools: An Everyday Lesson*, peer violence, defined as the number of children who report having been bullied in the last month or having been involved in a physical fight in the last year, is a pervasive part of young people's education around the world.

The report finds that approximately half of all students aged 13 to 15, or 150 million girls and boys, experience peer violence. This violence exists in every region of the world and in every community.

The report explains that the effects of peer-to-peer violence are unacceptably high on individual young people as well as on society as a whole. Violence decreases self-esteem, reduces attendance, lowers grades, and leads many children to drop out of school completely.

FROM BEING BULLIED TO MEDIATING CONFLICTS

Dzogovic said that during the time she was being bullied, a new group of peer mediators were brought into her school. She had never heard about the group and was admittedly skeptical. "At first I did not feel comfortable. I thought it was yet another group (that) would bully me," she said.

But this group was different. The group was organized by UNICEF and partner organization in Kosovo (SCR 1244) DOMOVIK, as part of a school-based violence prevention program. The peer mediators were student volunteers trained to resolve conflict at school, which were often cases of bullying and psychological abuse. They were also trained to refer more serious cases of violence to appropriate officials, including social welfare authorities and the police.

The peer mediators worked with school administrators, teachers, and the student council, as well as psychologists and education specialists. Dzogovic decided to join the group. During the first year of being a peer mediator, the bullying she was experiencing stopped. She also brought positive changes into more students' lives.

"When I joined, I found it to be a wonderful group and started to work on myself," she said. "I now put in extra effort when I see a child being bullied, and also suggest the child join the peer mediation team."

Over the last five years Dzogovic has helped end approximately 50 school-based conflicts or cases of bullying. She recalled one particular instance when she convinced two boys who had been fighting that physical conflict would not help. She said that she approached the situation as a friend, wanting to listen to both of the boys.

"That is how it was resolved," she said. Another important part of Dzogovic and the other peer mediator's work is visiting neighboring schools and re-enacting cases of bullying. During the reenactments, students learn how to identify bullying and resolve conflict.

So far, the peer mediation program has benefited at least 15,000 students in Kosovo.

— **Enlist help. Lots of it.** Whether you're writing letters to the editor, testifying at public meetings, or doing a nonviolent protest, keep asking for help from everyone you know. Send up flares for help in the sky as often as you need to. Keep reminding yourself that you don't need to do all this alone.

People love to help a great cause. And keep reminding yourself that young people have often been the first spark in a global and game-changing movement. In 1976, in South Africa, thousands of students marched through Johannesburg, eventually inciting a global action against apartheid. In Prague, in 1989, the peaceful young protesters of the Velvet Revolution brought about the free and democratic election of President Václav Havel.

— Be OK with learning new skills. To achieve your goals and be an effective change agent, you'll likely need to polish your existing skills or learn a few new ones to be an effective communicator. Remember how Parkland, Florida student Emma González had to quickly learn how to use the Twitter platform when she started to trend on it overnight? For any of us, the learning curves can be steep, so be patient. Sometimes you misspeak or stumble and need to correct your course. Sometimes you miss opportunities.

Often, you need to temporarily hit the pause button and polish your technique. As eloquent and inspiring a speaker as she is now, former First Lady Michelle Obama worked hard to hone her speaking skills during Barack Obama's presidential campaign in the Midwest, wrote speaker, writer and consultant Dana Rubin in a *Women of Influence* November, 16, 2018, online article, "3 Lessons from Michelle Obama About Finding Your Voice."

Rubin writes: "In the early days of her husband's presidential campaign, for the first time in her life, Obama was expected to do a fair amount of public speaking. She spoke in living rooms, bookstores, union halls, and retirement homes, energizing volunteers, and trying to win over leaders in the community."

But she was missing a script, talking points, or much advice, Rubin says. After her husband's victory in Iowa, the crowds got bigger and the stakes got higher.

So with campaign advisors, Michelle Obama studied videos of some of her public appearances with the volume turned down. She was able to spot any unflattering or undesirable facial expressions that she would need to control and got the support of a communication specialist to help sharpen her message and delivery. In time, that helped her feel a new ease, a new ownership of her voice, the article said.

— As professional public speakers do, practice your delivery and speaking style. Delivery matters. For her 17-minute speech at the Democratic National Convention in 2008, Obama "rehearsed and re-rehearsed until I could pace the commas in my sleep..." she said.

"She (Michelle Obama) found huge comfort in preparation. A teleprompter was set up in a corner of her office in the East Wing of the White House, and she used it," Rubin said. "She also pushed her scheduler and advance teams to make sure every detail of her public appearances went smoothly and on time.

"The truth is, rehearsing for a speaking event can be uncomfortable, in fact downright stressful. But the single biggest mistake speakers make is to wait until the last minute, or wing it," Rubin said. Wherever you're speaking, whether at a large event or advocating for yourself with an authority figure and others, here are a few more speaking tips to keep in mind:

— **Be clear, passionate and confident—but relatable.** Work to be conversational and natural. Sprinkle your message with stories and anecdotes.

— **Keep calm; stay collected.** Don't yell or get belligerent.

— **Take some pauses for your points to sink in.**

— **State without regrets or reservations what you believe in and know to be true.** Be bold and confident that you know what you know.

— **Ask for what you want.** Own your truth. Instead of saying, "You know, I kind of think" say, "I strongly believe that..." Do your homework, research, and imagine yourself confident and strong in your delivery, however you're speaking out. Own what you know.

— **Have fun and enjoy your presentation.** Be passionate. Be excited about your topic so others will.

Here are some final speechwriting tips that may be helpful if you're heading to a stage with your message. They come from Sarah Hurwitz, a former speechwriter for Michelle Obama.

"Speeches are often the canvases where a lot of things get worked out," said Hurwitz, as she shared her top three tips for speechwriting in a June 4, 2018 online post from Apex PR, "Top Speechwriting Tips from Michelle Obama's Former Speechwriter." They include:

- **Answer the following question: "What is the deepest, most important truth I can tell at this moment?" (Find a perspective to share.)**
- **Show, don't tell. (Use examples.)**
- **Talk like a human. (No one should ever use policy talk in speeches.)**

Another gem from Presidential candidate and U.S. Senator Kamala Harris, "So when you're standing up to speak? Remember, it's not about you...So if you were on the Titanic right now, and you know that you're about to sink, and you are the only one who knows, are you going to worry about how you look and how you sound? No, because the thing that is most important is that everyone knows what you know. Because they need to know what you know. So when you give your speech you know something and you have to share with the people the thing that you know." Share the thing you know.

— Be mindful of and honor people's time. Be brief, concise, and get to the point. When it comes to getting your message across, less is often more. A lot more. Whether in presentations, emails, voicemails or face-to-face meetings, be clear, engaging—and brief. People are swamped with deadlines and commitments these days. They really appreciate brevity.

So we made it through this organization section. Yay! Hopefully you're now even more fired up to advance your cause. After you've worked this hard, it's time to let go and hope for the best possible outcome.

FINDING YOUR VOICE IS OFTEN A LIFETIME JOURNEY

Changing someone's opinion and persuading people to act can often take longer than we want. Much longer, if you're working for a cultural sea change, to bust open stigmas, slay prejudices, or end discrimination, abuse, and bullying in an organization, or the culture at large.

But speaking out to spark that positive change is a huge first step. That is success itself. It truly is. And it encourages countless others to join you and get on your bandwagon. Bravo you! This is no small moment.

The fact that you spoke your truth is alone a major, huge victory. "If you join a fight for social justice, you may win or lose, but just by being part of the struggle, you win, and your life will be better for it," Howard Zinn said.

I am proud of you. Know that millions of people are waiting to be proud of you, once they hear of you. You showed up. And you were not quiet. Hear me cheering loudly for you!

And always remember: finding and using your one, true voice is a lifetime job. You are always practicing and perfecting how you use your voice for greater impact. Even the most seemingly rock-star courageous, powerful people are still finding they have to find their voices to share new truths to the world, often for the first time.

Ellen DeGeneres first opened up in 2018 about being sexually assaulted as a teenager. DeGeneres said she was inspired by the Senate testimony of Christine Blasey Ford, who said Supreme Court Justice Brett Kavanaugh sexually assaulted her when they were in high school.

DeGeneres went on NBC's *Today* to speak her raw and powerful truth, saying she was angry when people mock or don't believe abuse victims. "As a victim of sexual abuse, I am furious at people who don't believe it and who say, 'How do you not remember exactly what day it was?'" she said to *Today's* Savannah Guthrie in an October 5, 2018 interview. "You don't remember those things. What you remember is what happened to you, where you were, and how you feel. That's what you remember."

"I hope that I'm empowering women. We just have to not be quiet anymore."
— Ellen DeGeneres

DeGeneres said she feels it's important to use her voice and show as a platform to make a difference. "If anything, before I stop doing this show someday, I hope that I'm empowering women," she said. "We just have to not be quiet anymore."

In an interview with David Letterman that first aired on Netflix in May 2019, DeGeneres spoke out again and identified her former stepfather as the man who abused her when her mother wasn't home.

"I'm angry at myself because you know, I didn't, I was too weak to stand up to (him.) I was 15 or 16. It's a really horrible, horrible story and the only reason I'm actually going to go into details about it is because I want other girls to not ever let someone do that." She told Letterman that by coming forward she can inspire other women who "just don't feel like we're worthy, or we're scared to have a voice, and we're scared to say 'No.'"

ANYONE CAN BE AN ACTIVIST: A YOUNG MUSLIM WOMAN'S LEADERSHIP AND VOICE

Finally, if you're working on advancing a cause or issues, here's some incredibly wise, concrete advice from one of your peers. Keep remembering to get inspiration from one another, everywhere.

I am grateful that Aaisha Bhuiyan, who was Brand Contributor for *Forbes'* Civic Nation, granted permission to share her voice. Bhuiyan is also an ambassador for the United State of Women, working on the launch of the New York chapter. She grew up in Bangladesh where she began learning about religion, socioeconomic disparities, and the arts.

Her *Forbes* column, "Anyone Can Be an Activist," appeared on March 21, 2019:

"'Was media present at this event? Were you in any of the pictures? Please don't go next time. I worry for your safety,'" my mom told me on the phone. I come from a family of Muslim Bangladeshi immigrants, and moved to New York when I was six years old.

"After my parents' divorce three years later, I ended up moving back to Bangladesh. Thus began the back and forth of only seeing my mom in the summers and being raised in two very different cultures.

"I went to eight different schools across two continents and grew very interested in the socioeconomic differences within my communities. I was always asking questions and meeting fascinating people from all walks of life.

"My interactions with people kept me curious and always willing to learn. During my time at Penn State, I participated in panels and club meetings about community engagement, and when things took a more unfortunate turn, candlelight vigils (and multiple of them).

"Any time I'd tell my parents I attended such 'controversial' events concerning racially motivated discrimination or death, the conversation would always end with: 'Please don't go next time. I worry for your safety.' Because I am visibly Muslim (I wear a headscarf), my parents feared for my safety at such social events. 'What if things took an ugly turn?

"I COULD NOT STAY QUIET, SO I DIDN'T"

"'What if you get heckled, what if you get shot? Don't hang out with your Muslim friends too much. Especially if they have beards, that doesn't bode well with the West.' So unfortunate—when a person denounces characteristics of their own culture for fear of discrimination.

"While my mom played an integral part in building me into a strong woman, I'm saddened by the fear our society has instilled in her and thousands of other mothers like her. Men traditionally grow beards in Muslim countries. But before beards became a token of popular Western culture, brown men with beards were seen as threatening. This is something our men had to live with as a part of their identity before beards were 'cool.'

"Today, you can still find brown men shaving off their beards before big meetings. And unfortunately, this mindset stuck with my parents: If you have a beard, you and the people you associate with will be discriminated against. I haven't let this rhetoric discourage me from looking Muslim and being comfortable in my skin.

"I strongly believe that only when you are fully comfortable with yourself can you expect a foreign society to be comfortable with you.

"Following the 2016 presidential election, I felt it was imperative to stay involved in my school's social demonstrations. It was more important than it had ever been before. I found my Muslim roommate crying the morning after the election, fearing what would come next. Would people treat us differently now that we had put a president in office who said, 'I think Islam hates us?'

"I remember leaving the house that day feeling the weight of my headscarf for the first time. But, to my surprise, no one looked at me differently. Instead, I remember seeing a lot of long faces; some seemed almost defeated. There was a strange lull on campus, no one was talking. But we needed to talk. How else were we supposed to understand what we were feeling and move forward?

"I knew we needed to address the situation and educate ourselves on what other groups were feeling. My peers, professors, and members of the community got together one evening and discussed how people of color felt. We sat in a room trying to figure out where to start. What did activism even mean? It is too often misunderstood I had originally thought activism was taking to the streets in protest or tweeting about petitions to sign.

YOUR EXISTENCE IS ACTIVISM. YOUR REPRESENTATION IS ACTIVISM

"But I learned that there are different kinds of activism: Occupying space in your work fields, earning and owning your education, and using your voice in a meeting are all forms of activism. Standing up to verbal and physical assault on the streets is activism, but also, educating your racist uncle at the dinner table is activism. Your existence is activism, your representation is activism, and your allyship is activism.

"My senior year project, 'State of Mind,' became seeking creative expression from diverse perspectives in the college community, a community that had become my home. To me, art was therapeutic, and the combination of creating art with community building was the perfect way to heal my home. I paired with members of the community—the curator of a local art museum, a gallery, and a fellow peer, Alyssa—to bring to fruition a weeklong art exhibition addressing the socio-political situation in the country.

"I am no longer waiting around, I am unapologetically the change I want to see in the world." — Aaisha Bhuiyan

"Submissions were welcomed from artists but submissions from non-artists were encouraged; I wanted to create a space where our rawest emotions lived, especially from those who have never picked up a paintbrush. I believe if you feel strongly enough about a topic, you don't need skill to express it.

"The opening night was followed by three panel discussions hosted by my friend, Hamsa, who discussed being Muslim in today's America. One specific panel stood out to me, 'Constructive Activism,' in which leaders across various fields discussed how they were creating change in their own roles to better serve internal members of their community and to educate the non-members. Years later, our discussion on how to be constructive is really what influenced my thoughts below.

"Some may think an activist as a person holding up a protest sign, rallying against the perpetrators of hate. The Oxford dictionary defines activism as 'the action of using vigorous campaigning to bring about political or social change.' But campaigning is no longer the only route. There are ways you can be an activist in your daily life:

"Create Art: Hamsa's panel featured Amirah Sackett, a dancer in full clad hijab, choreographer, and teacher who uses dance to dispel misconceptions about Muslim women. The idea of using dance as a form of activism caught me off guard, but artistic expression is a valid and effective way to voice your opinion. Make art, communicate your views through a painting, song, or poem. Personally, I draw on the words of Swiss-French architect Le Corbusier, 'I prefer drawing to talking. Drawing is faster, and leaves less room for lies.'

"Participate in Protests or Peace Walks: Once, I expressed hesitation about participating in a protest, a professor told me, 'Just because you don't agree with something doesn't make it any less effective. Protests get results.' And I've learned to appreciate that by looking at American history—protests generate awareness and spread information. What have we achieved thus far with protesting, you may ask. I'll direct you here. 'Protest smart, don't be provoked, and stand up for what you believe in.'

"Teach: If you're a teacher, you're an activist. You're educating the leaders of tomorrow, in whose hands lie our future. Fight ignorance through them. And if you don't have a classroom full of students, teach yourself! Get a subscription to a newspaper online or offline— read from publishers that do not support your political or social ideologies, read from authors who do not look like you or sound like you. Seek out education about groups different from yourself. Exercise your mind, be aware of what's happening around you on a national and international level. Do it for yourself, be alert. Not only will you sound like you know your stuff, you will also actually know your stuff.

"Occupy Space in all Fields: The product of your career and work should reflect diversity. Post-panel discussion, I started to view activists as dancers, teachers, artists, poets, and philosophers. I also started to view people of color with a strong presence in the workplace as activists—your representation in every room matters. I am the only Muslim individual in my job.

"This may seem like a foreign concept to some, but I've struggled with imposter syndrome. It makes me feel like I don't deserve my success, or like I was just hired to fill a quota, especially because, I can't point to a single leader at most companies who share a similar ethnic/religious background.

"And that is why representation matters—the more we can put POC in leadership roles, the less we will feel like imposters. Let's occupy roles as scientists, business leaders, writers, artists, lawmakers, and more. People with the ability to create any little change in the world. I aim to be a leader in my industry as a woman, as a

Muslim, and then as a visibly Muslim woman in the garb.

"These examples only scratch the surface. Your activism is unique to what you stand for. My activism is in the way I carry myself, what I wear, what I read, the way I speak, the way I sit, the way I represent Muslim women in corporate America as an Ambassador for the United State of Women."

CHAPTER SEVEN
KEEP GOING HIGH:
PUSHBACK IS PART OF THE PROCESS

"No matter what happened, I had the peace of mind knowing that all the chatter, the name-calling, the doubting—all of it was just noise. It did not define me. It didn't change who I was. And most importantly, it couldn't hold me back."

— Michelle Obama

If you own your own voice and claim your truth, will you be criticized or get pushback? Discover haters you didn't even know existed? For sure. Or at least, some of the time.

Just as surely as the sun comes up each day, it seems to be a law of nature that if you speak from your heart, there will be people who will clap back.

But know this: when someone mocks you, tells you to shut up, or be quiet? When you have a feeling in your gut that they're trying to intimidate you into silence? Rain on your parade? Throw shade on you? That may be the exact moment you've got to find a way to speak. Loudly. And keep speaking.

My experience is that when others have tried to pressure me, even bully me, into staying silent? That's the exact moment when I knew I had something powerful to say that needed to be said.

LIFE IS NOT A POPULARITY CONTEST. YOU DON'T NEED TO PLEASE EVERYONE

At times like this, keep remembering: speaking your truth is not a popularity contest. Your goal is not to please or be liked by everyone. Your mission is to be strong and say what you have to say. Be heard. Get your needs met. Inspire a change. Let others know you care. Spark hope. Be who you are. Throw cold water on despair. Ignite action. Change a piece of the world.

You are not for everyone. And that's more than OK. "You are not a pretzel," tweeted writer Karen Salmansohn on December 13, 2015. "Do not twist yourself into who you think people want you to be just to make them happy, which then makes your soul feel all twisty like. Be who you are. Accept and love all your quirky aspects. Make your soul happy. Don't be a pretzel. Be the whole enchilada."

Be the star you're meant to be. Learn from the incredible Wé McDonald, a finalist on the show, *The Voice,* in 2016. Singer Alicia Keys said, "There is never going to be another person on the planet with a voice like Wé's." Watch her audition on *The Voice,* and it will blow you away.

But initially, McDonald was afraid that her voice wasn't good enough, because her speaking voice is dramatically different from her singing voice. Her speaking voice is far higher.

"So for anyone who has fear of being who they are, recognize who you are first. Recognize your good and bad qualities. That is the first step of getting better and then moving forward. And if someone doesn't accept you in your growth period that is not a welcome person to have...as long as you are forever yourself...you will feel much better." — Wé McDonald

"My biggest fear was what people thought of me. I was afraid they wouldn't like it (my voice)," McDonald said in our interview. "So I tried to be someone else. See I sang in bars and it was a problem for me because I had the two different voices, speaking and singing. I tried to make them match."

But it didn't work to try to be someone who she wasn't and strain to try and synch her two voices, McDonald said. "I got over that and saw that the only way to get over my fear was to present myself to people as genuinely as I could...And now, the thing I was fearful of, is what I am noticed for."

Just be yourself. Embrace all of you. Try to take off any masks you still wear and work to accept your strengths and your weaknesses.

Not everyone will get you. Or support you. Some people will always want you to be different. Quieter. Know your place. Fit in. Be less.

DO NOT TWIST YOURSELF INTO SHAPES TO PLEASE OTHERS

That's OK. They can exercise their freedom of speech. But do not let them stop you from standing up and speaking out. Do not let them make you small or snuff out your fire. Do not let them hold up much space in your amazing world. Keep reaching for the sun.

"Please do not twist yourself into shapes to please. Don't do it. If someone likes that version of you, that version of you that is false and holds back, then they actually just like that twisted shape, and not you. And the world is such a gloriously multifaceted, diverse place that there are people in the world who will like you, the real you, as you are," said Chimamanda Ngozi Adichie, author of the highly-acclaimed *Americanah*.

Amen, sister. If you are going to claim your own words and truth, anticipate that others, maybe authority figures, including your own parents, maybe friends or family closest to you, perhaps people you will never even meet—it's insane—will try to shun or shame you. Don't take any of it personally, as hard as that may be. Just keep doing you.

If you know your truth, don't let negative people stall your positive momentum. Stay woke and don't let the fear chase you away from what matters to you. I really like what this author recommends, "If you run from your fears, they will follow you. If you run straight at your fears, they will get the hell out of your way. Fears hate it when you do that," says Jen Sincero, *You are a Badass Every Day* author.

One of the best ways I've found to rise above my critics, the ones who will never know me and what makes me tick? I ignore them. And I let the sound of my own awesome sing louder. I am always open to legitimate criticism, kindly and respectfully offered. But when people toss out rude, even malicious comments? I let the glory of my own true voice rip. And make no room in my life for people who do not have my best interests at heart. You shouldn't either.

Remember to take good, extra care of yourself in all this, OK? Do what fills you up and renews you, whether that's listening to music, hanging with great friends, hiking, reading, etc. Being this brave isn't easy. Being a voice for change takes a lot of energy. It takes a lot of believing in yourself and knowing your worth.

Being a force for good can often be tough and a little lonely, at times. Especially if you're coming up against entrenched, dug-in, or super tough people and situations. So recharge yourself and do the things that fill you up, daily. Keep filling yourself up first so you can then go outward and work for more goodness.

Take a page, many pages, from *The Voice* finalist Wé McDonald and how she let the sound of her own unbelievable voice drown out the voices of her detractors. I'm playing *"Don't Rain on My Parade"* incessantly after interviewing McDonald—one of my most favorite interviews ever. She said it was one of her favorite songs from her show performances.

McDonald's on a mission "to perform my heart out," but also help kids stay whole and safe. And after learning how mercilessly she was bullied for three years in junior high, I am in awe at how this meteor is lighting up the sky. Here's some of her wisdom to light up yours.

A FINALIST FROM NBC'S *THE VOICE* REFLECTS ON WHY THE VOICES OF YOUNG PEOPLE STRIKE SUCH A CHORD NOW

McDonald: "I feel like our generation resonates with so many others because unlike past generations, we are relatable. I am honest and I don't pull any punches especially when it comes to life experiences. People tiptoe around certain issues, and I don't like to do that. I say, 'I struggle. We struggle. We can struggle together.'

"That is what touches people now. It's not easy to be as vulnerable. It's a hard thing to tell the truth. It's easy to be jaded because you don't know how someone will perceive your truth and what you've done and what you've been through.

"Or you're not sure how much truth to tell that is just in everyday life...and when you are in the spotlight you have to make sure whatever you do you do it right. I didn't know I was going to be a role model. But I know that is my role now. But I have to let people know that I am going to mess up. I am going to F--up a million times, but as long as I am honest and try to stay true to myself people will know it's OK."

After having a phenomenal experience with a lot of friends in elementary school, McDonald's middle school experience almost crushed her. "I never experienced a bigger school so I didn't know I'd been in a bubble before. I was bullied from 6th to 8th grade...It was not just physical, it was emotional and spiritual bullying. It got so bad that by 8th grade, I was just ostracized completely. I had nothing. I didn't have anybody. I went to a Christian school, and I always say my closest friend was Jesus."

The first week of school, McDonald said someone called her a "gorilla." Unbelievable.

"I had never been called any names or ugly things. I was very confused...I had long hair, really big hair, curly hair and I kept it in braids, and people kept pulling my hair and asking me if it was horse hair. I had glasses and acne and was chubby. I was an easy target. I was a textbook target. I was so taken aback at how they treated me...it was tough."

But McDonald found a friend, and they developed a good bond. But then bullies sabotaged that, too. "There were rumors going around we were gay. They also started a rumor that I was a boy and had a penis. That was the running joke."

So McDonald went back to having no friends, being isolated, so isolated, she sometimes ate lunch by herself in the bathroom stalls. Her school tried to hide or downplay the bullying. She reported it, regularly, to her parents. Her mom wanted her to switch schools, but McDonald refused to let the mean kids run her out of school. "I stayed and promised I would graduate. They would not take that away from me."

And she did. And when McDonald was getting ready to graduate from 8th grade, she went to an arts school. "I loved it and saw what an accepting audience was. Acting, singing and loving each other, we were like a big family. And I thought, 'Oh, my God, this is it.' I have to start writing and making music because the whole world cannot feel the way I felt for three years...I didn't know how big this would get in any way, shape or form...I just knew in my head that I wanted to help myself...

"I felt there was nothing I could do to fix any of the stuff going on, and the only thing I did know how to do was to write, and sing and dance and act...I said I love the arts, and that is my thing. I can rely on that. I can rely on my parents and my beautiful support system, thank God."

Through the nonprofit No Bully, McDonald has toured the country to help kids stand up to bullying and find their authentic voices. She's also written a book, *The Little Girl with the Big Voice*, about a young girl who courageously embraces her uniqueness and discovers her true voice, no matter what others think or say.

No Bully is a nonprofit organization that ignites compassion to eradicate bullying and cyberbullying worldwide. Founded in San Francisco, No Bully was started by a team of educators, psychologists, and lawyers committed to building a kinder and more compassionate world through ending the crisis of bullying, harassment, and violence in schools and online.

"There are so many beautiful qualities within you, so don't let anyone take your light away or make fun of you. That is THEIR problem and has absolutely nothing to do w/you. If someone is making fun of you, they either fear or envy you or do not like themselves. Turn to someone you trust and ask for help." — Wé McDonald

Since its founding, No Bully has had over a 90 percent success rate eliminating bullying in schools and has served over 326 schools, 202,000 students and 16,000 teachers by partnering with institutions, families, parents, and students to teach the healthy use of power by empowering voice, compassion toward others, and inclusivity. (See No Bully's concrete tips for using your voice to bust bullying at the end of the book in additional resources.)

McDonald's recommendations if you're being bullied: "Sometimes you have to put your foot down and tell someone to genuinely back off. In that kind of tone. As you stand up and are confident you have to say, 'Leave me alone and if you come up to me again, I will have teachers and staff with me, so do not bother me again.' If stupid things happen, yeah, just ignore that. But if you do need to take action in other ways or go to another school, do that. I took a different route, so find out what works for you.

"Always go to someone you trust, regardless of what you are going through, there has to be an adult, family or close family friend you trust. Tell them what is happening. And remember that middle school is not your entire world. I promise you that 80 to 99 percent of the people around you now will not matter in two to three years, in any way, shape, or form.

"There are so many beautiful qualities within you, so don't let anyone take your light away or make fun of you. That is their problem and has absolutely nothing to do with you. If someone is making fun of you, they either fear or envy you or do not like themselves. Turn to someone you trust and ask for help."

Never let haters rain on your parade, OK? Take a cue from the Parkland, Florida students. They were mocked by many and hate-tweeted by President Trump. "Nobody wants to be hate-tweeted, especially by the president," said Oprah Winfrey. "So it's not a comfortable thing I think for anybody on social media who's had somebody say something about you that you didn't feel was true. But I believe that you meet any kind of negativity in your life, that you meet it with light."

Keep shining big. Keep glowing like the brilliant light you are and that many love. And trust that your light is so bright it's not meant to stay in the shadows. That's too narrow for you. Use criticism to polish and strengthen you because you're destined for great things.

HOW AN 11-YEAR-OLD GIRL IGNORED THE BULLIES AND BECAME A GLOBAL SENSATION

And I know that sometimes your own peers don't understand and ridicule you. Just keep believing in yourself and beaming the hope. UK student Nadia Sparkes was only 11 when she began to inspire the world by collecting litter in her bicycle basket on the way to school. She proudly wore a school uniform made from recycled plastic bottles.

Even as her leadership was praised, Sparkes was soon ridiculed "Trash Girl" by bullies. Look at what she did. She went higher. She turned the "Trash Girl" slur on its head and embraced the nickname because Sparkes said it made her feel "like a superhero." Awesome.

Her Facebook page attracted thousands and inspired people to pick up three pieces of litter each day. Creative Nation created a cartoon superhero for her, saying, "Trash Girl rules," and encouraging schools to display the cartoon to encourage other kids. Incredibly awesome.

And Sparkes continued to pick up trash, saying it was the right thing to do, "I'm doing something to protect the world they also live in. It's everyone's job. We are all responsible for keeping this world safe, instead of believing that it's always someone else's job," she said about the bullies.

Due to her unwavering dedication, Sparkes also continued to receive the highest praise. Former British Prime Minster Theresa May presented her with a Points of Light Award on April 12, 2019. "Through your 'Trash Girl' campaign you are changing attitudes on littering and inspiring thousands of your fellow students to take action," May wrote to Sparkes. "You are sending a positive message that we should all take responsibility for looking after our local environment, and should feel very proud of the difference this is making."

ACTORS EMMA WATSON AND CHADWICK BOSEMAN RISE ABOVE CRITICISM AND PUSHBACK

Look around you. Find a few people who came of age with some of the same issues as you. See how they are speaking and coping with pushback and criticism.

Take actress and humanitarian Emma Watson. One of the first young people to stand up for feminism, gender balance, and ending the wage gap, including in Hollywood, she was verbally attacked online.

When she starting talking about women's rights in 2015, Emma said that within 12 hours she was receiving online threats. She shared this admission during a live Facebook Q&A session for the HeForShe equality campaign in March, 2015

Her family was understandably concerned about the threats, she said. "I think they were really shocked, and one of my brothers in particular was very upset."

The threats turned out to be a hoax, and Watson was galvanized even more to speak out. "It's funny, people were like, 'Oh she's going to be so disheartened by this.' If anything, it made me so much more determined. I was just raging. It made me so angry that I was just like, 'This is why I have to be doing. This. This is why I have to be doing this.' If they were trying to put me off, it did the opposite."

"Call me whatever you want. It's not going to stop me from trying to do the right thing and make sure that the right thing happens." — Emma Watson

In 2016, Watson spoke out again saying that when she speaks up as a feminist for women's rights and gender balance, some critics labeled her a "feminazi." Her response was brilliant: "Fine. Call me a 'diva', call me a 'feminazi', call me 'difficult', call me a 'First World feminist', call me whatever you want, it's not going to stop me from trying to do the right thing and make sure that the right thing happens. Because it doesn't just affect me." Her comments appeared in an April 3, 2016, *Esquire* article, *"Esquire Meets Emma Watson."*

And there's too much at stake to be quiet or intimidated, Watson said. "Whether you are a woman on a tea plantation in Kenya, or a stockbroker on Wall Street, or a Hollywood actress, no one is being paid equally.

"I've had my arse slapped as I've left a room. I've felt scared walking home. I've had people following me. I don't talk about these experiences much, because coming from me they'll sound like a huge deal and I don't want this to be about me, but most women I know have experienced it and worse."

Believe in your own worth and magic, even if others fail to see it. Don't let others stop you from doing what you feel is right. Even if it has repercussions, as it did for actor Chadwick Boseman. Here's another story from his commencement address at Howard University.

Boseman told the graduates that he once used his voice to share his concerns about his first television role on a soap opera.

SPEAKING OUT CAN BE YOUR DEEPEST SOURCE OF STRENGTH IN TIMES OF STRUGGLE

Boseman said he felt he had to speak up about the role—a stereotypical young, black man with a violent streak, pulled into the world of gangs. "I was conflicted, because this role seemed to be wrapped up in assumptions about us as black folk. The writing failed to search for specificity. Plus, there was barely a glimpse of positivity or talent in the character—barely a glimpse of hope," he said.

But when he spoke up, Boseman was fired, which is another example of how setbacks can happen when you're standing up for what you believe. They just do. That's the nature of struggling for what you want. But as disappointing as these setbacks can be, they can help you get even better clarity about what matters, Boseman said in his commencement speech.

"What do you do when the principles and standards that were instilled in you here at Howard close the doors in front of you? Sometimes you need to get knocked down before you can really figure out what your fight is. And how you need to fight it," he said in a May 13, 2018 National Public Radio piece, "Black Panther' Star Chadwick Boseman Lauds Student Activism In Howard Commencement."

Speaking out can sometimes be bruising, but, more often, it will be your deepest, undeniable source of strength. It will save you and help you soar. That has, without a doubt, been my experience.

I will never forget my first speaking engagement after my first book celebrating prominent women's life achievements, passions, and spirituality was released. I was on a Denver panel at a major book conference. There may have only been 75 people in my breakout room, but it felt like 750. I was so nervous. My legs, arms, and mouth felt like they weren't even attached to me. My stomach? I was glad I'd not eaten much lunch that day.

But when it came my turn to speak on the panel, I felt wobbly, but a bit more confident once I got rolling. I was articulate and relatable, I hoped. I felt I was speaking authentically about my book, which I loved.

All was going well...and then. The last person spoke, a theologian with multiple religious titles. Though my book featured standout role models like Jane Goodall, Elizabeth Kubler Ross, former First Lady Betty Ford, Madeleine L'Engle, and other stellar women, this man scoffed at my stories and called me a "flake" in a highly arrogant tone.

I was mortified. I was incensed. I saw people in the audience react in disbelief. And I had to quickly decide what to do. So I ignored him. I just kept answering questions from the audience. I didn't give that person the satisfaction of seeing my discomfort. My stomach was running in worried circles on the inside, but I was Wonder Woman on the outside. And I kept answering great questions from audience members. This person was not going to steal the thunder of my book and the amazing stories in it. I just kept beaming my truth.

You know what? There will always be people who are triggered by your truth, for whatever reason. Don't let their behavior throw you off course. Take the high road, and keep your eye on the glorious prize. Celebrate the sound of your own voice.

People in the audience came up to me afterward. "Wow, can't believe that happened. But you came off the larger person, good for you!" one woman said. And my book? *Embracing Our Essence: Spiritual Conversations with Prominent Women* went on to be a bestseller, receive widespread national news coverage, inspire an Oprah show, and prove to be a well-timed spark in the women's spirituality movement.

It also was the catalyst for my growing courage. And speaking and advocating for what I believe on a larger landscape and stage. I will always be grateful.

In the end, how and when you use your voice is your right and your responsibility. Only yours. Don't let haters harden your good, strong heart. Just don't. Keep your heart soft and open. Stay brave. Be strong. Hang with the people who are in love with good things. Stay kind. Help others. Speak your truth. In all this lies your power.

CONCLUSION

KEEP SPEAKING: YOUR WORDS MATTER

"Speak. You cannot be afraid. You cannot be afraid to share your deepest thoughts, your opinions, your beliefs, the ideas you have rolling around the corners of your mind. You cannot be afraid of what people will say, or if they will agree. You are entitled to your own feelings, own convictions, own words. And regardless of what happens when you say them aloud, you need to do just that—speak them to life, bold and strong.

"What if someone told you that your words are important, would you write them then? Fill pages? Change hearts? Well, I'm telling you now. What you have to say matters," Marisa Donnelly wrote in an April 22, 2016, *Thought Catalog* essay.

I echo Donnelly and all the other wonderful voices in this book. What you have to say matters. YOUR VOICE MATTERS. And I thank my lucky stars that your path somehow led you to this book. I see your generation's greatness and am inspired by it. Please let others see it. Let your gifts and voices shine.

Take your hearts full of grace and souls generated by love and be as great as you can possibly be. Not perfect. Just authentically, wonderfully you. (Hugs from your author here.)

Greatness, as Wé McDonald has shown, is about just being yourself. "You are enough. You are more than enough, and regardless of what anyone says about you, you are beautiful. You are smart. You are strong."

I hope that these pages have helped you find and enjoy, even more, the sound—and power—of your own amazing voice. I also hope this book and the people in it help you stand taller and stronger. You may be one, but you are one of many. And if you speak, you might light the spark for which others have been waiting a very long time. And your spark will help them stay hopeful and find their kindred people.

We can't wait for anyone else to speak for us. We no longer have the luxury of hoping "others" will find their courage and speak first. If we feel a nudge, a sense, a fire in our soul, or a hand at our back pushing us forward, then we have to be the ones to speak up. This is your moment. This is our moment. Let's seize these moments, together, to be all we can be.

Keep remembering to surround yourself with people who believe in you, your story, your cause, and who have your back. All the way, not just when it's easy or popular. Align with people who understand the magic— and the mission—of what you have to say. And speak at the top of their lungs for your right to say it.

Spread hope. Be hope. Speak hope. And as you inspire others to speak, stand with them, too. Share this book with them. Help them when they need a boost. Together, we form a Your Voice Matters movement of people who will keep speaking, advocating, and working for change. One voice at a time.

And finally, never, ever doubt how much your collective words matter. We are in deep gratitude to you and your generation. As I said at the beginning of this book, we see you and can't wait to hear what you have to say.

My respect and love to each of you. This book is dedicated to you.

SOME FINAL RESOURCES AND YOUNG VOICES:
HOW TO STAND UP TO HATE TALK WITH YOUR OWN WORDS

If you don't speak up, you're surrendering part of yourself. You're letting bigotry win."

— Bob Carolla, spokesman for the National Alliance for the Mentally Ill.

If you want to stand up to hate talk, which is, sadly, on the rise, here are some great tips from the Southern Poverty Law Center's guide, *"How to Respond to Everyday Prejudice, Bias and Stereotypes."* SPLC developed the book to help teachers address the hate speech, bullying and bigotry that have risen in schools since 2016.   https://www.splcenter.org/

"The point is to draw a line, to say, 'I don't want you to use that language when I'm around,'" said Bob Carolla, spokesman for the National Alliance for the Mentally Ill. "Even if attitudes don't change, by shutting off bad behavior, you are limiting its contagion. Fewer people hear it or experience it."

Here are some SPLC ideas that can help you find the words you need when you need them.

Script some messages and/or responses and rehearse what you want to say. Having memorized responses to inappropriate language and behavior can be super helpful because it's hard to know what to do in the moment, as one teacher observed: "You're tongue-tied. Someone has said something biased that makes you uncomfortable, or even angry. You want to say something, but you're not sure what to say. It happens almost daily.

"Maybe it's one of your students. Or it's a colleague. Or an administrator. And maybe you laugh along—a forced or awkward laugh—because you don't want to be rude." But don't let hate have the last word, she urges.

Script some ready responses that will work in a variety of moments, such as:

"That offends me."

"I don't find that funny."

"I'm surprised to hear you say that."

So you can speak up, but also open a conversation, you also can ask questions, the guide recommends, like, "What do you mean by that?" or "Why would you say something like that?" and "What point are you trying to make by saying that?"

Practice appropriate responses in advance. Memorize them. Have them ready for the next moment. "The most important thing is to say something," said Deb Nielsen, a middle school teacher in Durango, Colorado. "Don't let these kinds of put-downs pass. Put yourself out there, and you will make a difference."

Nielsen offered her own set of standard responses:

"Did you mean to say something hurtful when you said that?"

"Using that word as a put-down offends me."

"Using that word doesn't help others feel safe or accepted here."

HOW TO BUST BULLYING: TIPS AND IDEAS FROM NO BULLY https://www.nobully.org/

The nonprofit No Bully offers these recommendations to prevent and deal with bullying: Schools have a responsibility to make their campuses bully-free. Speak to someone at school who you trust and ask for their help. If your school does not help you, try out some of these ideas:

• When you are bullied, it is easy to give your power away and feel helpless. Hold your head up and stand tall.

• Remember that you have the right to be respected for who you are. Targets of repeated bullying sometimes believe that the putdowns and insults they receive are actually true. Don't! It may be hard to change the way that other students treat you, but you do have control of what you think about yourself.

• Find an ally. Tell a parent, a neighbor, a relative, a friend, or your school counselor. Being bullied feels many times worse if you try to endure it alone.

• Find a Facebook group for students around bullying. If you search Facebook you will find several groups you can join.

• Create an anti-bullying campaign team. Find other students that care and invite them to form a campaign team to make your school bully-free. Use your first meeting to figure out what types of bullying are most frequent at your school. Use the No Bully definitions of bullying.

• Write a petition that calls on your school principal to end bullying at your school. You, or your campaign team, can create this online at www.change.org.

• Bring No Bully to your school. You, or your parent or a teacher can request that No Bully comes to your campus.

• Call a help line. If there is no one that you feel safe talking to, and you have thoughts that your life is helpless, call the Trevor Helpline immediately at 1-866-4-U-TREVOR (1-866-488-7386).

HOW TO BUST THE SILENCE ON LONELINESS, ANXIETY, AND DEPRESSION

We all have times when we have to ask for help or acknowledge that we're anxious, lonely, or depressed. "It's okay to not be okay," said Lady Gaga, whose foundation has a peer-to-peer mental health program, Teen Mental Health First Aid, at work in some U.S. high schools. It's OK to admit you need help.

YOUNG BRITISH AUTHOR LIBBY PAGE SPEAKS LOUD ABOUT LONELINESS

And sometimes, it takes as much courage to say out loud that we're lost or lonely as it does to speak on a stage, you know? That's why I'm so grateful for young British author Libby Page, whose hit novel, *The Lido*, beautifully explores loneliness and the power of connections.

Page has bravely spoken and written about her own experience with loneliness, which has helped bust the stigma around a topic she says "can feel something like a dirty secret."

In an April 30, 2018, *Grazia* article, *"We Shouldn't Feel Ashamed of Loneliness,"* Page wrote, "When I left home for university, I was the only person from school to move to London. I arrived knowing no one and immediately felt overcome by homesickness mixed with an aching sadness. I had this irrational feeling that no one in the entire city would want to be my friend, ever.

I can now look back on and recognize that feeling as loneliness.

"But at the time it took a while for me to admit I wasn't strange, or sick, or a failure: I was lonely."

Luckily, after a few months, Page made a new friend. And she continues to make many new friends—and readers—by being admirably real.

The Lido's main character also deals with panic attacks and on April 7, 2019, Page posted on Facebook: "Like Kate in *The Lido*, I have experienced panic attacks throughout my life, starting when I first moved to London. Luckily, I now only get them very infrequently (swimming and exercise in general has really helped) and when I do it's mostly when I'm in crowds.

"Being among too many people can make me feel like everything is pressing down on me. And yet one of my favourite places in London is Columbia Road flower market, a place where you have to shuffle among the crowds, pressed up amongst strangers. I visited there today and it made me realise it's the one place where crowds don't bother me.

"You just have to accept that you aren't getting anywhere fast and give in to it, and enjoy it even. And everywhere you look are flowers and happy people clutching big bouquets.

"Writing about 'The Panic' in my book really helped with my own anxiety and I really hope that if you've read it the descriptions of panic attacks feel real, as they were largely based on personal experience. Thank goodness for things like swimming and beautiful flowers—for me both amazing antidotes to feeling anxious."

MY Q&A WITH *THE LIDO* AUTHOR LIBBY PAGE

ME: You have busted the stigma around loneliness more. For those who are still afraid and ashamed to admit that they are lonely, what advice would you give them? Why does talking about it help?

LIBBY PAGE: The very nature of loneliness means that it makes us feel as though we are alone and cut off from others, and perhaps that what we're going through is unique to us. We feel lonely and yet we perceive others around us as having full and exciting social lives. As though everyone else is at a party we haven't been invited to. And yet research shows us that loneliness is a huge issue experienced by people of all ages, from all backgrounds. So you might feel lonely, but you are certainly not alone. That knowledge has helped me to speak more openly about my own experiences of loneliness. And as soon as I did start talking about it, I was overwhelmed by how many people—whether in my own life or readers of my book or articles—told me it's something they have felt too. So to anyone who is feeling lonely I'd say to try and keep this in mind – no one is immune to loneliness and so there is no shame in feeling this way. I also think there are practical things that can be done to help beat off loneliness when it hits—I've found that volunteering, joining a sports club and just trying to become more of an active member of my community have really helped me. Don't be afraid to share with those around you that you're feeling this way. I've found that as soon as I opened up about my own loneliness, that's when I started to feel less alone.

ME: In terms of using one's voice, can you address why it's empowering and helps one stay hopeful and forward-looking in a world that can often look bleak and dreary?

LIBBY PAGE: I certainly found that writing about my own experiences of loneliness in my novel was empowering. Just writing about things I had been through, and turning them into fiction, helped me to take control over my low feelings in a way. It helped me also to step back and look at it more objectively. I had been through a period of loneliness but that didn't make me a bad or antisocial person. I've also found it empowering to write about loneliness through journalism too because it felt like a way of helping to break down the stigma around loneliness and to reach out to others who might be feeling low.

ME: Can you share a story from your own life of someone who you inspired? Someone who said you made a difference in their lives when you found the courage to speak out about your own loneliness?

LIBBY PAGE: I have certainly had numerous people get in touch to say that they have been through periods of loneliness too and my words helped them feel like that was okay, and that they weren't alone. Because my novel is about finding community through swimming, I've also had lots of people get in touch to say that reading it has inspired them to take up swimming or join a local club. I think sport can be such a social thing and a great antidote to loneliness.

A WINDOW INTO NEXT-GENERATION VOICES: REFLECTIONS SHARED BY WEBBER MIDDLE SCHOOL STUDENTS, FORT COLLINS, COLORADO

It helps to hear how your peers feel, so you know how much you have in common. Here are a few voices I was grateful to gather from a northern Colorado middle school. I thank each of these students for sharing their awesome writing for this book.

Anonymous:

"A Time I Didn't Use My Voice"

"There are so many things I think about saying to my friends/sharing to a class that are poetic or meaningful, but I just can't muster up the courage. It might be because I am self-conscious, and I hate the feeling of a classroom of eyes staring at me—but I get this feeling around individual people, too, more commonly people I don't know very well and want to get a good impression of.

"I tell myself not to care about what other people think, but it's a struggle to just suddenly stop thinking about that. That's why I show more of who I am or what my thoughts are in writing because then when people read it (or if it's a journal entry when I read it) they heard exactly what I'm too anxious to say out loud. An example is birthday cards. I can edit and revise what I want people to hear, but when I talk I can't take it back. There is no eraser for that."

Jesse:

"I know I wish I had a rewind button for my life so I could stop myself or so I could speak up. But I can't. I can't do anything anymore. And that's what tears me up inside. Because I want to. But I don't know how to."

Anonymous:

I am:

From the spirit of the vast blue ocean.

From the wind whistling past the

rollerblader's ears

From the jagged edges and smooth curves of
a mountain

From the sapling's first breath

From the everyday lurches and jolts

From the high peaks of Mt. Everest and the
depths of the Mariana Trench

From the wink of the eye

From the twitch of the mouth

From the eyes of the hawk

From the shudder of curtains

From the trail of dust

From the swish of the shark's tail

From the chirp of the mourning dove

From the layers of the grey cloud

From the voice of the French horn

From the ring of the piano keys

From the bark of the mutt

From the raise of the eyebrow

From the slice of the nut cake.

Josephine:

When asked to write what she would say if she had a microphone under her chin and would tell the world what she knows and feels as a middle school student:

"I think global warming has a huge effect on our generation and future generations. Growing up in this world, there are so many more environmental issues because some generations before us didn't care. As I was growing up, there were already some animals extinct. For future generations they might not get to see other animals."

When asked, "How do you use your voice?"

Josephine:

"I have used my voice in writing. I try to send a message about things that really matter to me. When I feel a strong emotion, I use my voice to try and talk about how I feel. I always voice my opinion when something matters to me.

I do not stand up for myself when I need something. I am always trying to hide it if I need something. When I do need something, I don't tell anyone, and I try and find a way I can find what I need myself. It is hard to write about this because I usually talk about things I care about."

Emma:

"One time I used my voice is when this guy at my table called one of my friends a word that offended him (my friend)... I began to ask him why he did that. I told him to stay away from that word because it's offensive and rude. One time that it took me a while to stand up for myself was when I got bullied by my best friend who I was friends with for six years. At first the things she was saying weren't bad, so I ignored it. It then started getting bad as she was cyberbullying me. I decided to talk to my counselor and mom but it had been going on for a month and a half."

A FINAL GREAT RESOURCE

As you're using your voice for good, check out communities like The International Congress of Youth Voices, an international organization that showcases young voices around the world.

Here's some background: The International Congress of Youth Voices unites and amplifies the ideas and energy of young people around the world. It was founded in 2018 by author and activist Dave Eggers and nonprofit leader Amanda Uhle.

The goal of the Congress is to ensure that teen voices are heard anytime issues that affect them are being discussed in the media and in government.

The Congress's landmark inaugural meeting in 2018 in San Francisco convened 100 extraordinary teen writers and activists from 27 countries. The Congress's second gathering takes place 2019 in San Juan, Puerto Rico.

Congress delegates are high school and college students, ages 16 to 22, who have taken an active role in making their communities stronger and more inclusive. Their accomplishments, ranging from founding nonprofit organizations to leading grassroots civic efforts in their classrooms and schools, are all impressive.

Delegates are selected to represent diverse backgrounds, perspectives, and geography, as well as a continuum of accomplishments, to build mentorship opportunities between older and younger delegates.

At annual gatherings, youth delegates meet and organize together and learn with and from leaders like civil rights icon Rep. John Lewis, the founders of the Women's March, novelists like Edwidge Danticat and Chimamanda Ngozie Adichie, noted journalists, business leaders, activists, and more.

ABOUT THE AUTHOR

Susan Skog is an author, freelance journalist and speaker. She's written seven other nonfiction books for adults. Susan's also written for leading magazines and news organizations, including *AARP, The NY Times, Forbes, Science, Huffington Post, Hello Giggles, Today.com, Family Circle,* and others. As a former nonprofit communications leader, she rallied support across the developing world for girls' education, safe water, maternal health, jobs, and poverty relief. Susan lives in Fort Collins, Colorado and loves to travel, hike in the mountains, and enjoy friends, family, live music, and her sunflowers.

Photo Credit: Mary Pridgen

CPSIA information can be obtained
at www.ICGtesting.com
Printed in the USA
LVHW030034160223
739591LV00003B/577